Uniforms of the Armies at Waterloo

Volume 4
The French Army

As Drawn by
Charles Lyall
1894

Authors:	Markus Gärtner & Markus Stein
Translation:	Richard Sanders
Layout:	Stefan Müller
Publisher:	Zeughaus Verlag GmbH Knesebeckstr. 88, 10623 Berlin
Phone:	+49 (0)30-315-700-30
Email:	info@zeughausverlag.de
Internet:	www.zeughausverlag.de

Printed in European Union, 2022

All rights reserved.
Reproductions, translation, photographic reproduction, including extracts, are forbidden. Storage and distribution including transfer onto electronic media like CD-ROM etc. as well as storage on electronic media like the Internet etc. are not permissible without the express written permission of the publisher and are punishable.

© Zeughaus Verlag GmbH, Berlin 2022
ISBN: 978-3-96360-044-9

Introduction

This fourth volume concludes the series on the "Uniforms of the armies at Waterloo". This series provides the reader with a comprehensive compendium that presents all the units involved in the campaign of 1815 and each volume is accompanied by the artistic plates of Charles Lyall.

This volume deals with the French Army under the command of Napoleon I, the opponent of the Anglo-Allied and Prussian armies addressed in the three previous volumes. Napoleon succeeded in mobilizing a powerful army after his return in April 1815 from his first exile. He was able to draw on experienced soldiers and officers who had served in the Bourbon army, but he also called up veterans and inexperienced recruits, whose supply of uniforms and weapons posed a great challenge to the French commissariat. With a total of 70 plates, some of which also show units of the French Imperial Guard, which no longer existed in 1815, the reader gets a good impression of the appearance of the French Northern Army.

In addition, we have taken up the narrative of the Battle of Waterloo begun in the first volume and continue it here to its conclusion, the defeat of Napoleon and the retreat of the French troops towards the French border. As before, some contemporaries give a picture of the events, and in addition, two more maps from Siborne's *"Atlas to History of the Waterloo Campaign"* will help the reader to follow the course of the battle.

Finally, at the end of this small series, we would like to thank the man without whom this publication would not have been possible. The managing director of the Zeughaus Verlag, Mr. Stefan Müller, has not only provided the artistically successful and impressive plates of Charles Lyall in their entirety, but he has also given us, as commenting editors, the chance to supplement these plates with texts on the organization and uniforms as well as descriptions of the battle. We look forward to the opportunity to develop further publications in this form with him, and now wish to give this completed work the reception it deserves.

Markus Gärtner & Markus Stein

The Battle of Waterloo on 18 June 1815 (continued)

The description of the Battle of Waterloo in the first volume of this series was halted with the failed attack of the French d'Erlon Corps on the Anglo-Allied center. The corps' soldiers, flooding back, were able to reorganize behind the advancing Lobau Corps. The central battlefield was thus quiet until about 3:00 p.m., with only the French Reille Corps, which had been fanning out at Hougoumont chateau, engaged in more intense fighting.

La Haye Sainte farm , which had already been attacked during the d'Erlon Corps' assault, lay forward of the Anglo-Allied line. The farm was defended by troops of the King's German Legion and later by Nassau infantrymen, and from 3:00 p.m. it was attacked again more forcefully by French infantry. These infantry attacks continued until about 5:00 p.m., then the cavalry attacks gave the defenders of La Haye Sainte a brief respite.

French Cavalry Charges

The French infantry's unsuccessful attacks on the Anglo-Allied center between Hougoumont and La Haye Sainte convinced Marshal Ney to destabilize the enemy forces by a massive cavalry attack. Due to the renewed attacks on La Haye Sainte, the British soldiers retreated in an orderly fashion, which was misinterpreted by Ney as their disintegration and he ordered a cavalry charge.

To this end, the two cuirassier divisions of the Milhaud Reserve Cavalry Corps were brought forward at about 4:00 p.m., joined on their left flank by the Guard Light Cavalry under Lefebvre-Desnouettes. Eight regiments of cuirassiers and the Guard Chasseurs a Cheval, as well as the Red Lancers *(Lanciers Rouges)* of the Imperial Guard, approached the Anglo-Allied line between Hougoumont and La Haye Sainte. The Anglo-Allied line, located behind the ridge and not visible to the French, immediately formed up in square formations. This initial attack by ten French regiments of over 4,800 men was supported by up to ten batteries of cannons, which shelled the enemy line before the actual mounted attack. In this attack, the cavalrymen overran the Allied guns, so that Wellington was unable to use about half of his artillery at this point in the battle.

British Ensign Rees Gronow vividly describes the impression the attacking French cavalry made on the Anglo-Allied units:

> „... the very earth shook under the enormous mass of men and horses. I never shall forget the strange noise our bullets made against the breastplates of Kellermann's and Milhaud's cuirassiers, six or seven thousand in number, who attacked us with great fury. I can only compare it, with a somewhat homely simile, to the noise of a violent hail-storm beating upon panes of glass.
> The artillery did great execution, but our musketry did not at first seem to kill many men; though it brought down a large number of horses, and created indescribable confusion. The horses of the first rank of cuirassiers, in spite of all the efforts of their riders, came to a stand-still, shaking and covered with foam, at about twenty yards' distance from our squares, and generally resisted all attempts to force them to charge the line of serried steel ...
> Nothing could be more gallant than the behaviour of those veterans, many of whom had distinguished themselves on half the battle-fields of Europe.
> In the midst of our terrible fire, their officers were seen as if on parade, keeping order in their ranks, and encouraging them. Unable to renew the charge, but unwilling to retreat, they brandished their swords with loud cries of 'Vive l'Empereur !' and allowed themselves to be mowed down by hundreds rather than yield. Our men, who shot them down, could not help admiring the gallant bearing and heroic resignation of their enemies."

The cavalry, scattering between the squares of the Anglo-Allied infantry, did not succeed in breaking them, so that at about 5:00 p.m. the second wave of the cavalry charge began. Additional regiments of the Kellermann Reserve Cavalry Corps and the Guards heavy cavalry were added to this attack, thus nearly 9,000 horsemen rode against the Allied forces. But even this intensified attack could not break the steadfastness of the squares. French horsemen who got behind the infantry lines ran into counterattacks by Allied cavalry, especially the Dutch-Belgian Collaert Division. Wellington led Allied troops directly on the spot during this critical phase, as he was at times in the square of the second battalions of the 30th and 73rd Regiments.

Two decisive factors made the cavalry charges a major tactical mistake. The first was the failure to destroy the enemy guns, which had been overridden during the initial charge. The French cavalrymen carried little or no nails to spike the firing holes of the British guns. Thus, after the cavalry had retreated, the Anglo-Allied gunners, who had taken refuge in the squares, were again able to operate their guns and, above all, to fire on the last attack of the French Guards.

The second mistake lay in the lack of support for the attack by advancing infantry. Although the Bachelu Division and the Tissot Brigade of the Foy Division were ordered forward after the second attack, the Adam Brigade, ordered forward by Wellington, was able to repel the attack.

Thus, the attempt to break the Allied position by means of concentrated cavalry attacks ended in the early evening at about 6:00 p.m.. The remnants of the French cavalry retreated exhausted and could not be used decisively in the further course of the battle.

With the advance of the Bachelu Division and the Tissot Brigade west of La Haye Sainte, the attack on this farm was again intensified. Due to the defenders' lack of ammunition and the spreading fire, the French succeeded in capturing La Haye Sainte between 6:00 and 6:30 p.m..

The Prussian Attacks on Plancenoit

The Prussian units under Blücher had been advancing from Wavre since the beginning of the Battle of Waterloo, and at about 4:30 p.m. they met up with the first brigades of Losthin and Hiller to the east of the fighting. Napoleon opposed them with units of the Lobau Corps to avoid weakening his troops engaged in attacks on the Anglo-Allied line.

By 5:30 p.m., Bülow had assembled his entire corps of about 30,000 men and was able to begin attacking the French right flank. At 6:00 p.m., when the French cavalry finally ceased its attacks on the Allied line, the murderous battle for the village of Plancenoit began, costing some 11,000 wounded and dead on both sides by late evening.

The attack was initiated by the shelling of the French defenders by Prussian artillery at about 6:00 p.m. The Losthin and Hiller brigades with about 6,500 men attacked the French infantrymen in and around Plancenoit, still supported by French guns in the village. They succeeded in capturing the village and Napoleon had to march the entire Young Guard Division of over 4,700 men to prevent the southeastern flank of the French army from collapsing. The Guard Infantry managed to recapture Plancenoit in a man-to-man fight, but the Prussian Bülow Corps, now fully engaged in the battle, managed to retake the village by just after 7:00 p.m.

An impression of the battle in Plancenoit can be obtained from the regimental history of the Prussian 15th Infantry Regiment, published by Dörk in 1844, which took part in the attack on the village as part of the 16th Infantry Brigade Hiller:

> *"After 6 o'clock in the evening the attack of the village of Plancenoit, strongly occupied by the enemy Sixth Army Corps, was undertaken by the 16th Brigade; our two musketeer battalions proceeded at the assault pace against the village on the right. This maneuver, as the brigade report says, was executed with the greatest calm, as on the training ground, and succeeded in spite of the fiercest resistance of the enemy infantry. Our regiment and the 1st Silesian Landwehr Regiment, overcoming all difficulties and with considerable loss by cannister and smallarms fire, penetrated as far as the churchyard in the middle of the village, which was surrounded by a very high wall; the enemy, however, kept to the houses and hedgerows to the left of the latter and, despite all efforts, could not be driven from there. A fierce battle ensued in close proximity; at 15 to 30 paces they fired at each other without any part giving way or wavering ... and our regiment undertook it with the second attack on the village. This too succeeded after a fierce resistance, the village was conquered and a lot of enemy Guards were slain or captured in man-to-man combat."*

Napoleon had to detach two more battalions of the Old Guard from his last reserve, which, supported by the regrouping Young Guard units, regained possession of the village at 7:30 p.m. with a bayonet charge. The French troops were able to hold Plancenoit for at least another hour, until the failure of the last attack by the Guards on the Anglo-Allied troops started the general retreat. Between 8:00 p.m. and 8:30 p.m., the Prussians, now attacking with fourfold superiority, were finally able to capture the village and begin pursuit of the retreating French.

The Guard's Attack on the Anglo-Allied Line

After the French forces' so far unsuccessful attempts to break Wellington's Anglo-Allied formations, Napoleon personally led his last reserve into the field, namely five battalions of the Middle Guard and three battalions of the Old Guard. He handed over the command of the southern, now French-held, La Haye Sainte to Marshal Ney, who led the battalions - each of them led by a general of the Imperial Guard - into the plain between Hougoumont and La Haye Sainte.

The French attack on Wellington's reorganized formations along the ridge, especially those of the British Adam, Maitland, and Halkett brigades posted from west to east, began about 7:30 p.m. The French Guards marched in square formation toward the British lines, the five battalions of the Middle Guards in the front line, the three battalions of the Old Guards behind them. Between the battalions, a battery of Guard horse artillery advanced to shatter the Allied troops before the decisive thrust of the Guard infantry. French line units, following just behind the attacking Guard infantry, also advanced around La Haye Sainte and east of Hougoumont.

Marshal Ney lost his fifth horse in this attack during the battle and continued to lead the Guardsmen on foot. Within less than half an hour, the attack collapsed under the energetic volley fire of the British units formed up in line. The two Middle Guard grenadier battalions advancing on the right side of the attack were able to come within 40 yards of the Halkett Brigade's regiments and were then brought to a standstill by the combined fire of the infantrymen and artillery. The chasseur battalions advancing to the west of the grenadiers failed to spot the British Guards who were ordered by Maitland to lie down behind the ridge and were allowed by the French to come to within about 25 yards and then engaged them with volley fire.

Captain H. W. Powell of the 1st Foot Guards described the moment of the French Guardsmen's surprise and wavering:

> *"They [the French Guard] continued to advance till within fifty or sixty paces of our front, when the Brigade were ordered to stand up. Whether it was from the sudden and unexpected appearance of a Corps so near them, which must have seemed as starting out of the ground, or the tremendously heavy fire we threw into them, La Garde, who had never before failed in an attack suddenly stopped. Those who from a distance and more on the flank could see the affair, tell us that the effect of our fire seemed to force the head of the Column bodily back.*
> *In less than a minute above 300 were down. They now wavered, and several of the read divisions began to draw out as if to deploy, whilst some of the men in their rear beginning to fire over the heads of those in front was so evident a proof of their confusion, that Lord Saltoun [...] hollered out, 'Now's the time, my boys.' Immediately the Brigade sprang forward. La Garde turned and gave us little opportunity of trying the steel [of the bayonets]."*

The Adam Brigade, west of the British Guards, now executed a left turn to form a right angle with the Maitland and Halkett Brigades. They primarily took the battalion of the 4th Guards Chasseurs à Pied advancing to the west under flanking fire, halting their attack. With this, the last of the five Guard battalions attacking in the first wave also faltered and, like the other battalions, began to retreat. The line units attacking from La Haye Sainte were also swept away by this retreat, and the front of the French Northern Army thus collapsed shortly before 8:00 p.m. The three battalions of the Old Guard from the second wave of the attack were able to maintain their square formations but were unable to halt the general retreat. They retreated in an orderly fashion, and in some cases were subjected to withering direct fire at close range – including General Cambronne with the second battalion of the 1st Guards on foot, who shouted at Colonel Halkett of Hanover the famous words *"La Garde meurt mais ne se rend pas!"*.[1]

The general retreat of the French ended one of the most famous battles in world history, which led to Napoleon's renewed abdication and his exile on St. Helena. Over 50,000 men lost their lives or were wounded on the battlefield.

---

1   "The Guard is dying but is not yielding!"

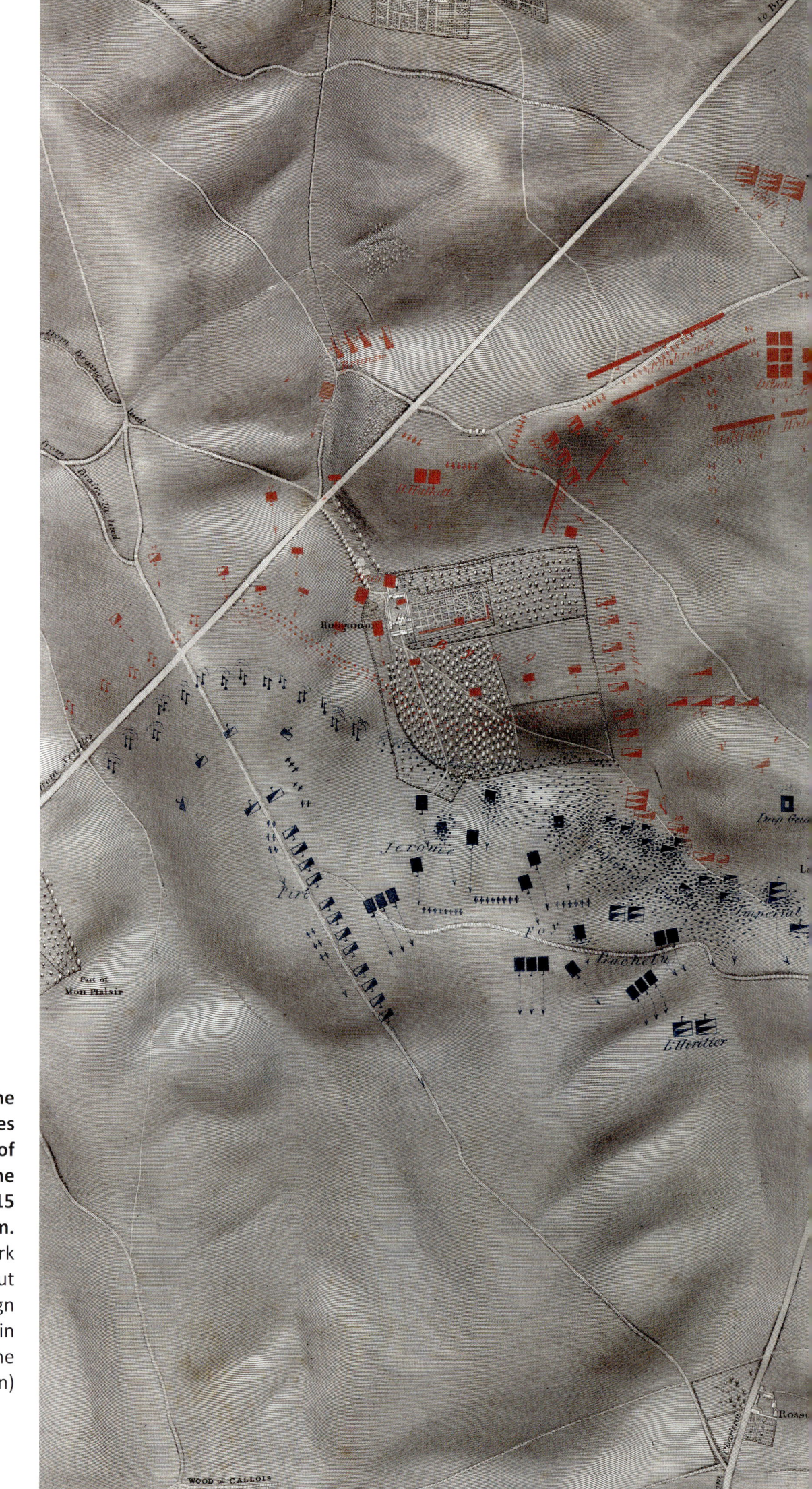

Positions of the opposing armies at the Battle of Waterloo on 18 June 1815 about 7:45 p.m.
(Map from the work by W. Siborne about the 1815 Campaign that appeared in 1844, from the author's collection)

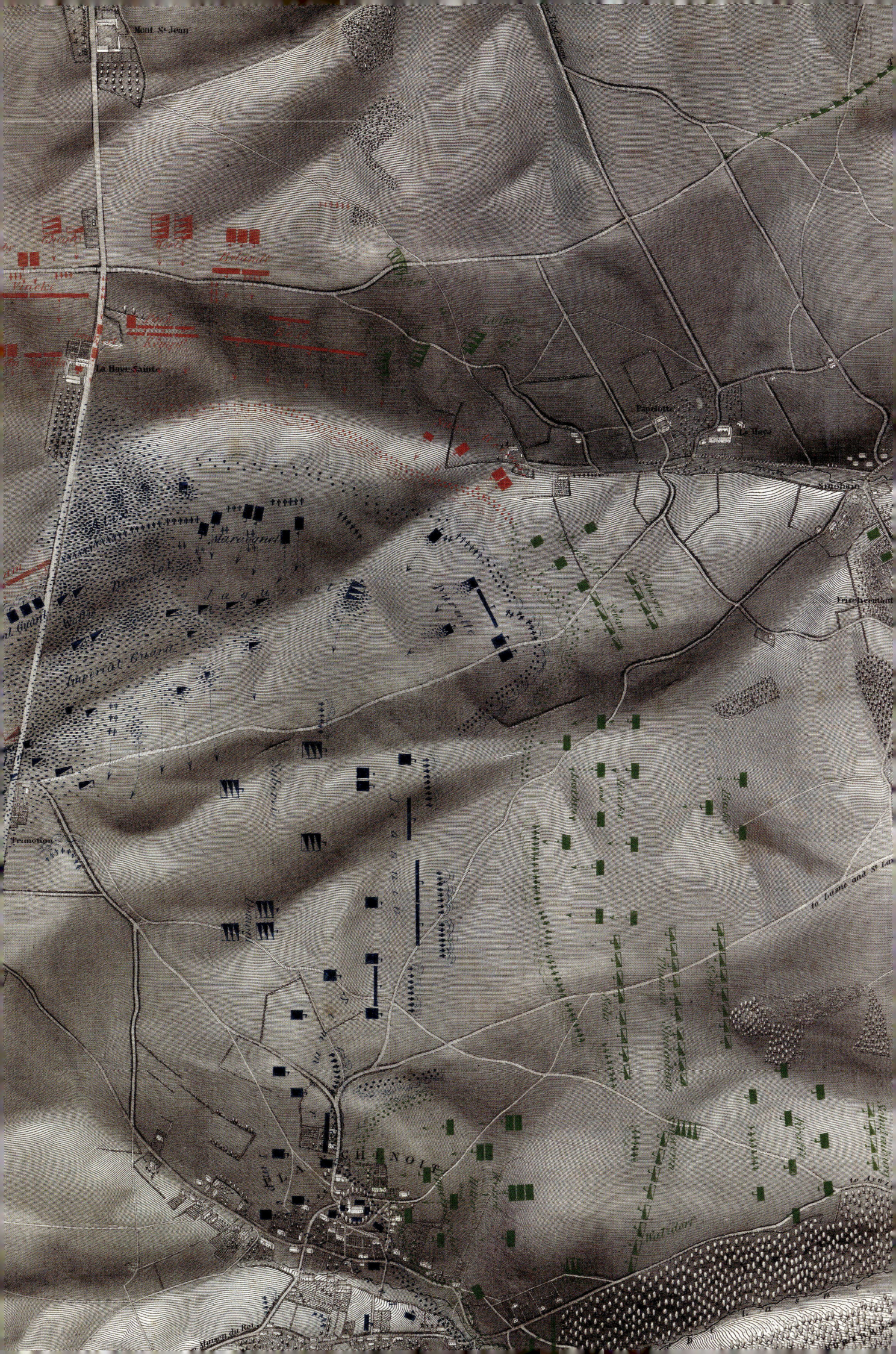

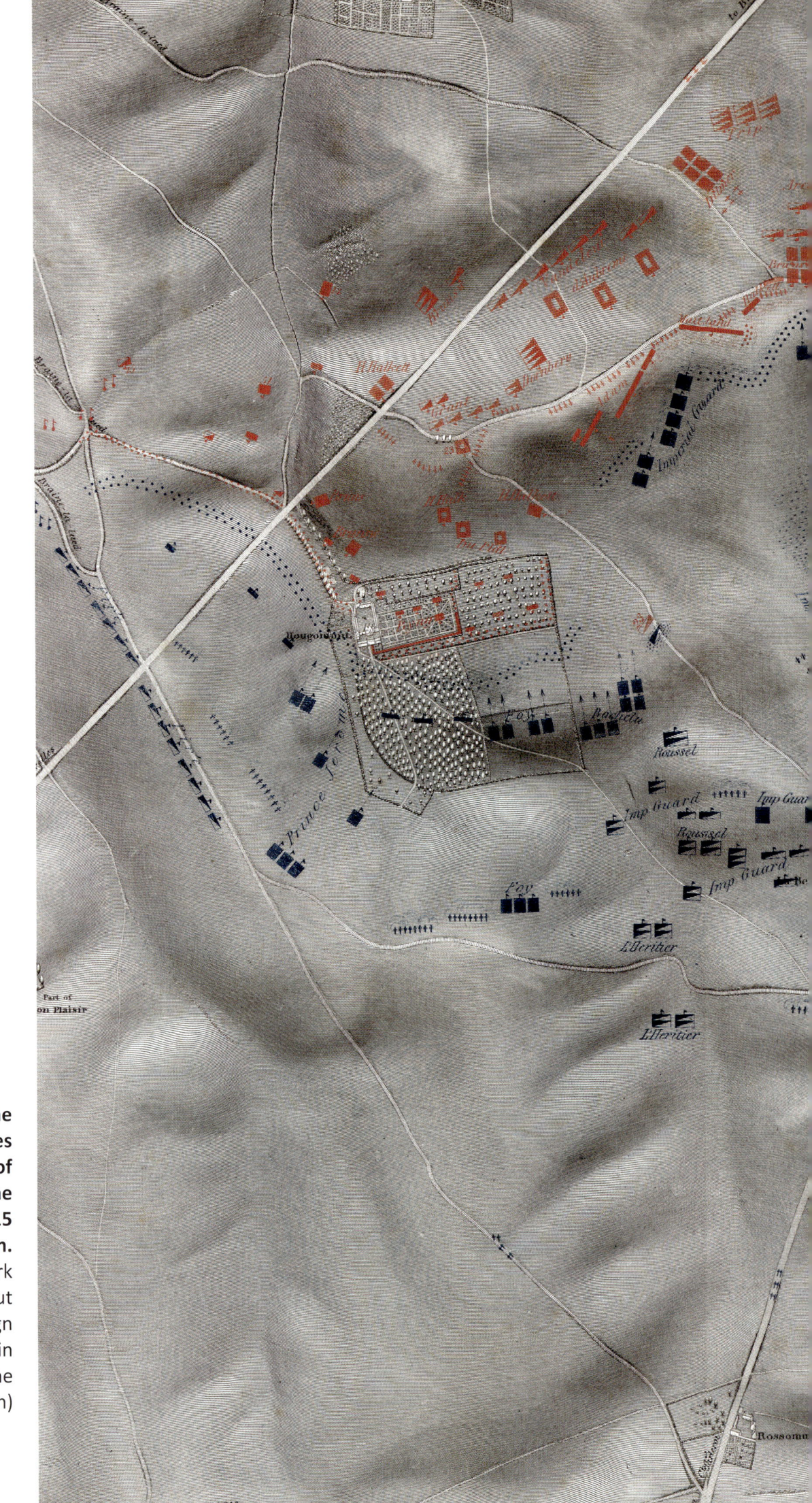

Positions of the opposing armies at the Battle of Waterloo on 18 June 1815 about 8:05 p.m.
(Map from the work by W. Siborne about the 1815 Campaign that appeared in 1844, from the author's collection)

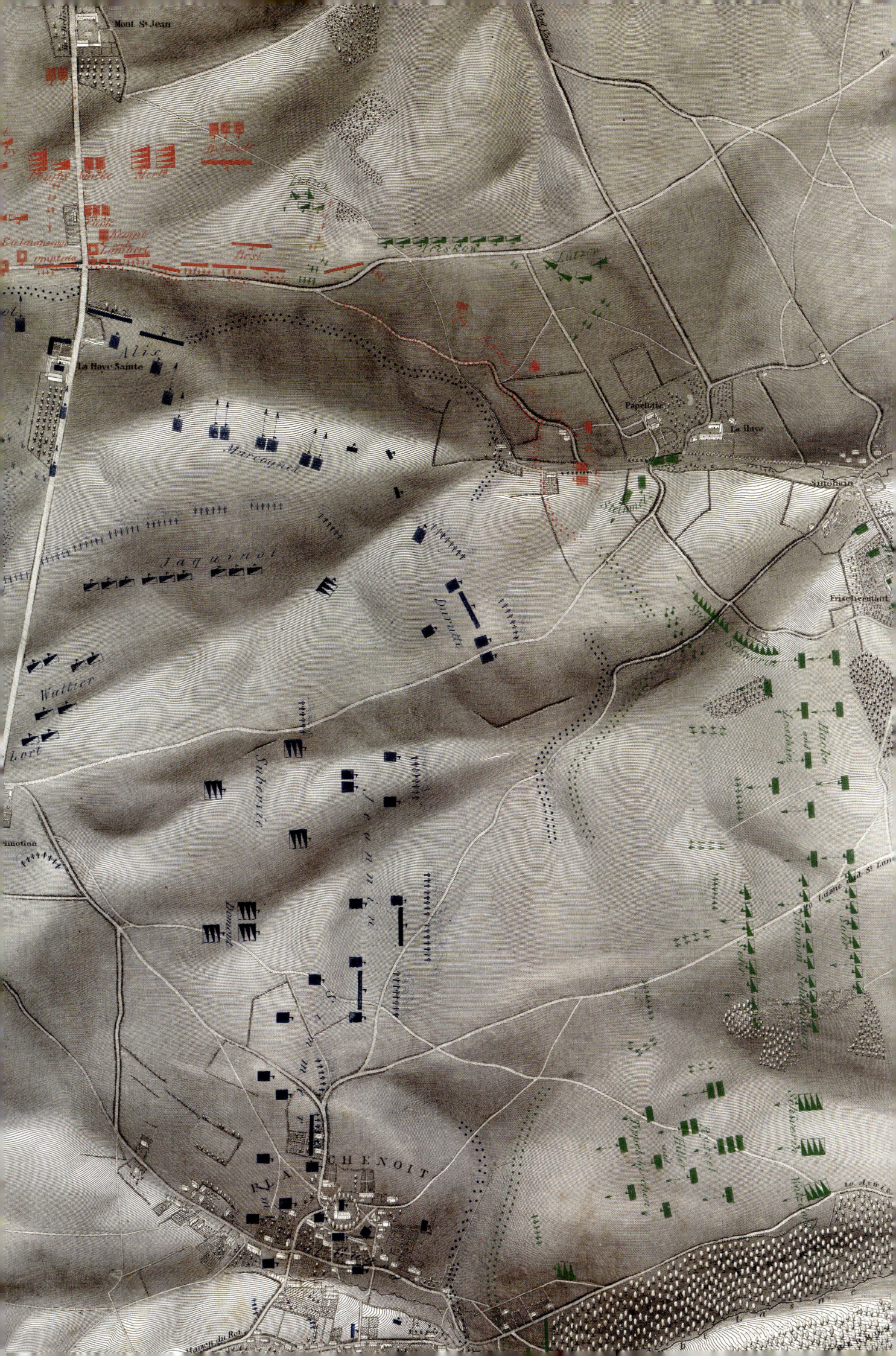

THE FRENCH FORCES' ORDER OF BATTLE, 1815

The following Order of Battle lists the units that were at Waterloo, excluding those that were under Marshal Grouchy at Wavre. Most infantry regiments had two battalions in action; where this was not the case; the number and strength are given in parentheses. For cavalry, the number of squadrons is always given. In addition, the strength of the units on 18 June 1815 is given in parentheses. In the listing of the Guard units, the addition "of the Guard" was omitted; only the attached regiment of Marine artillery was not a Guard unit.

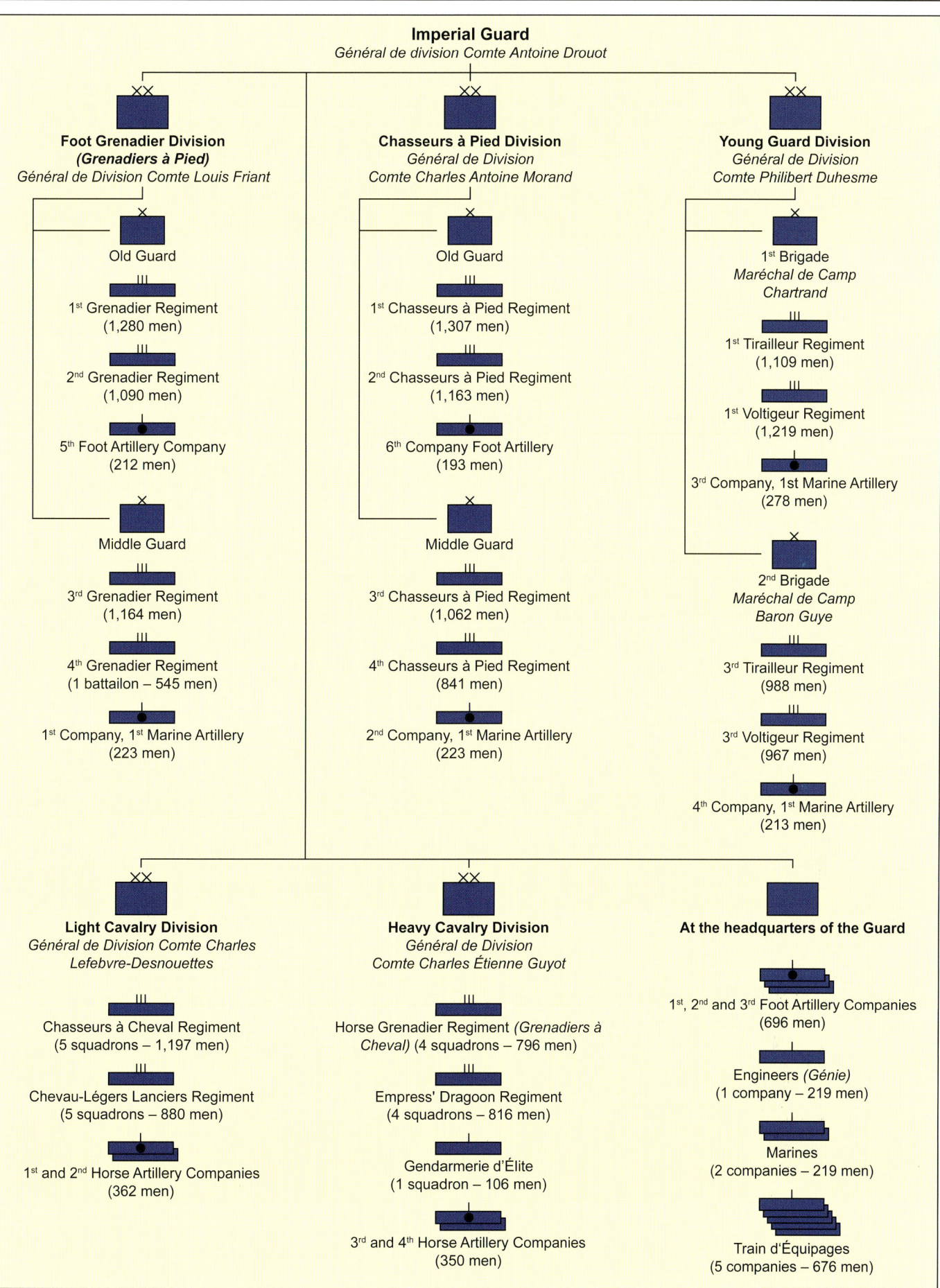

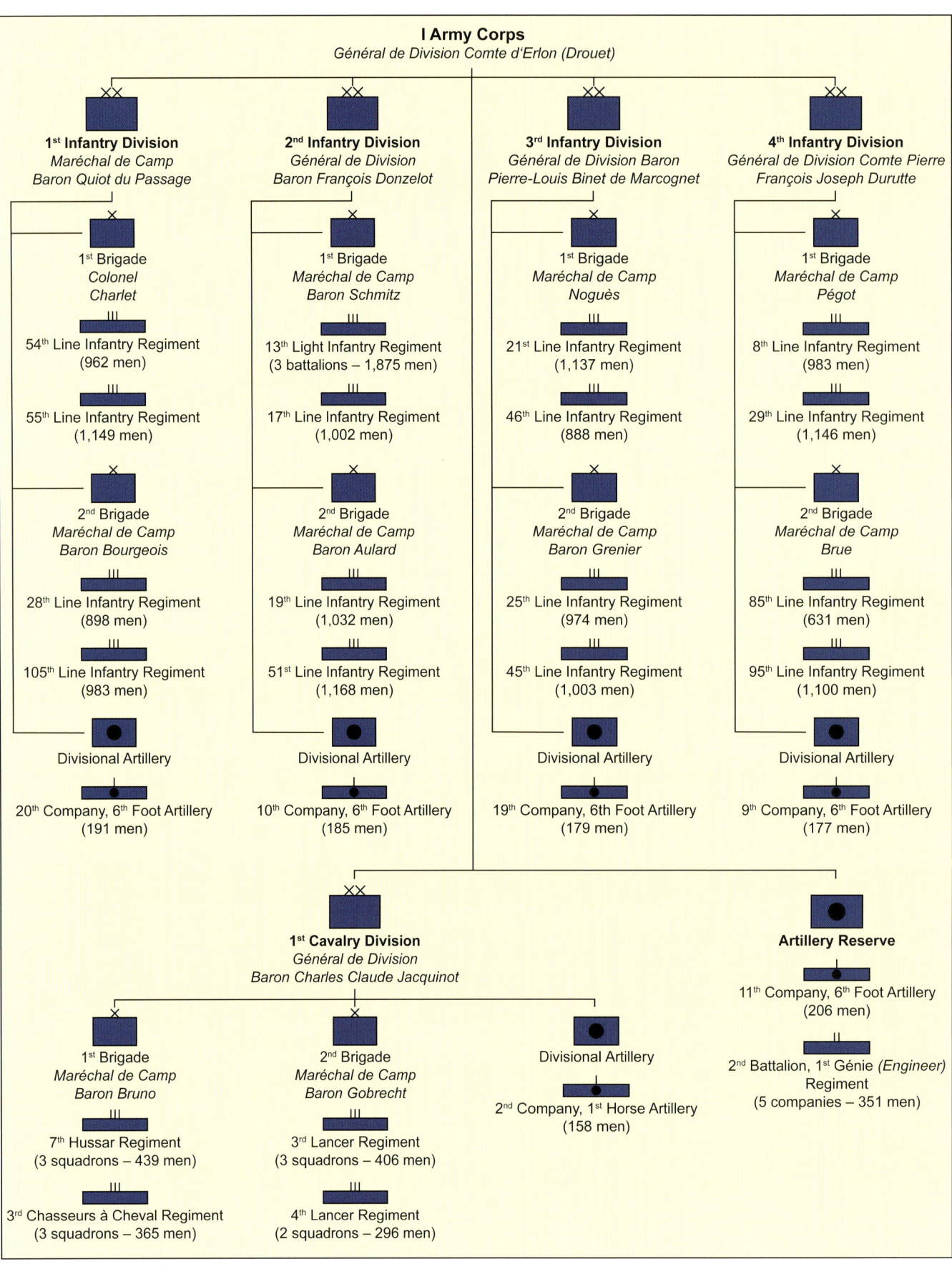

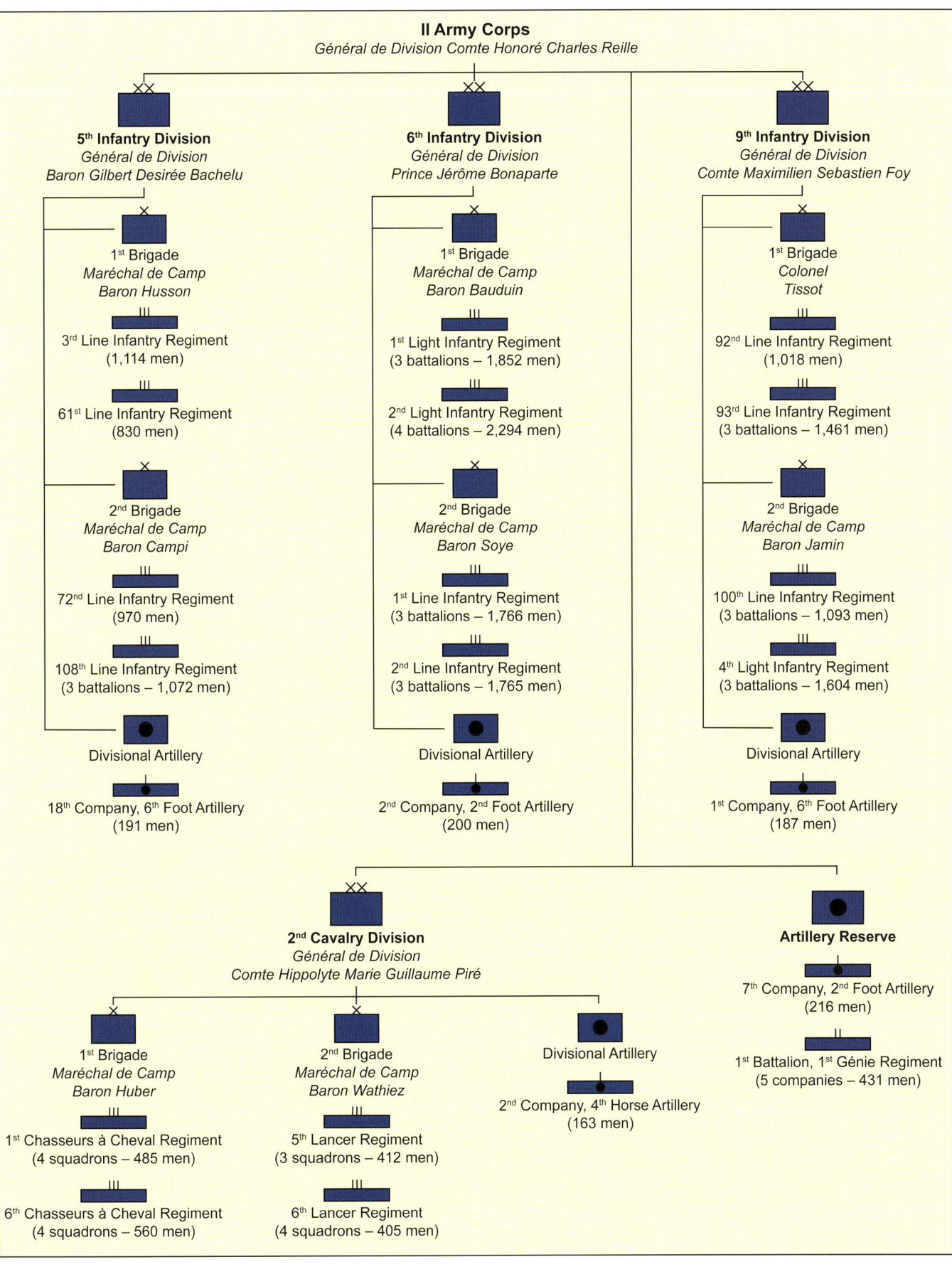

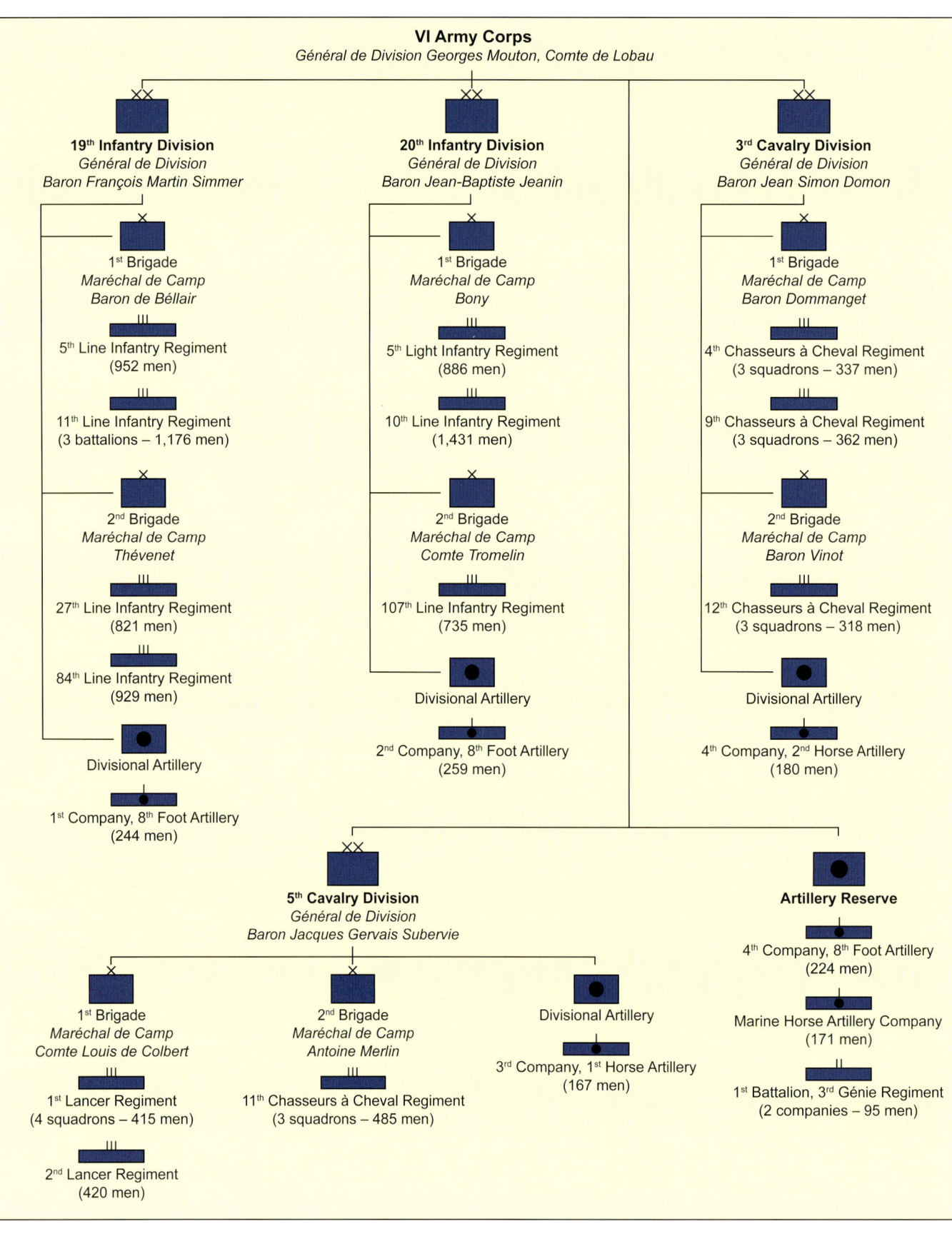

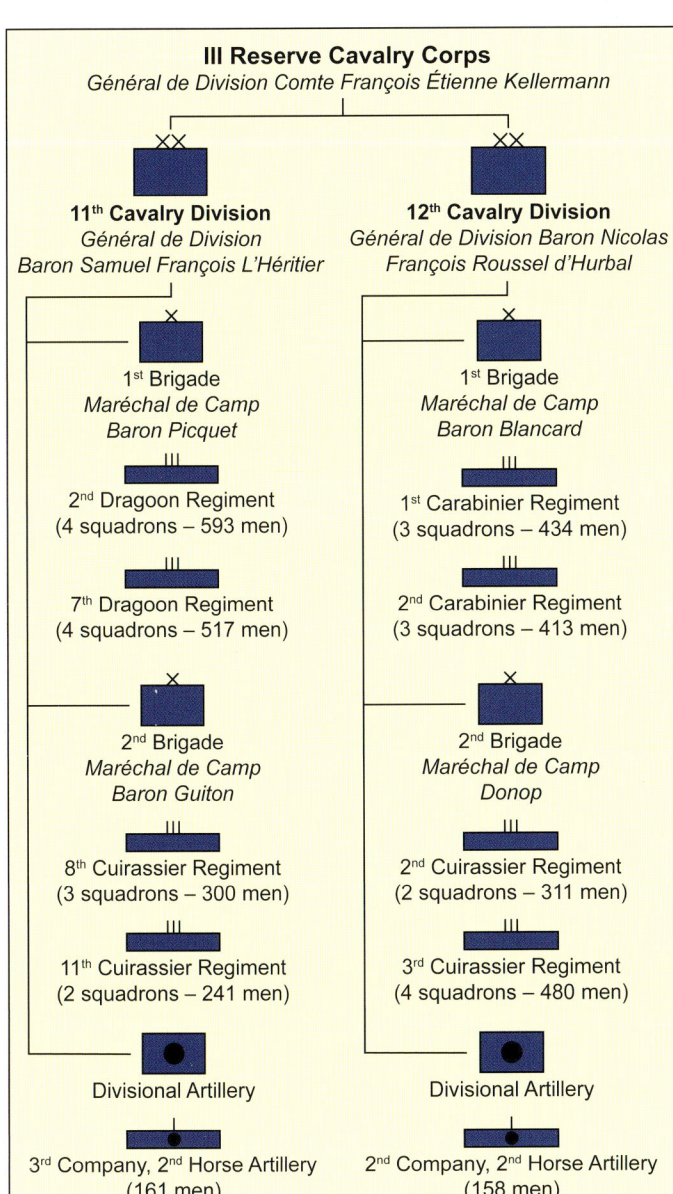
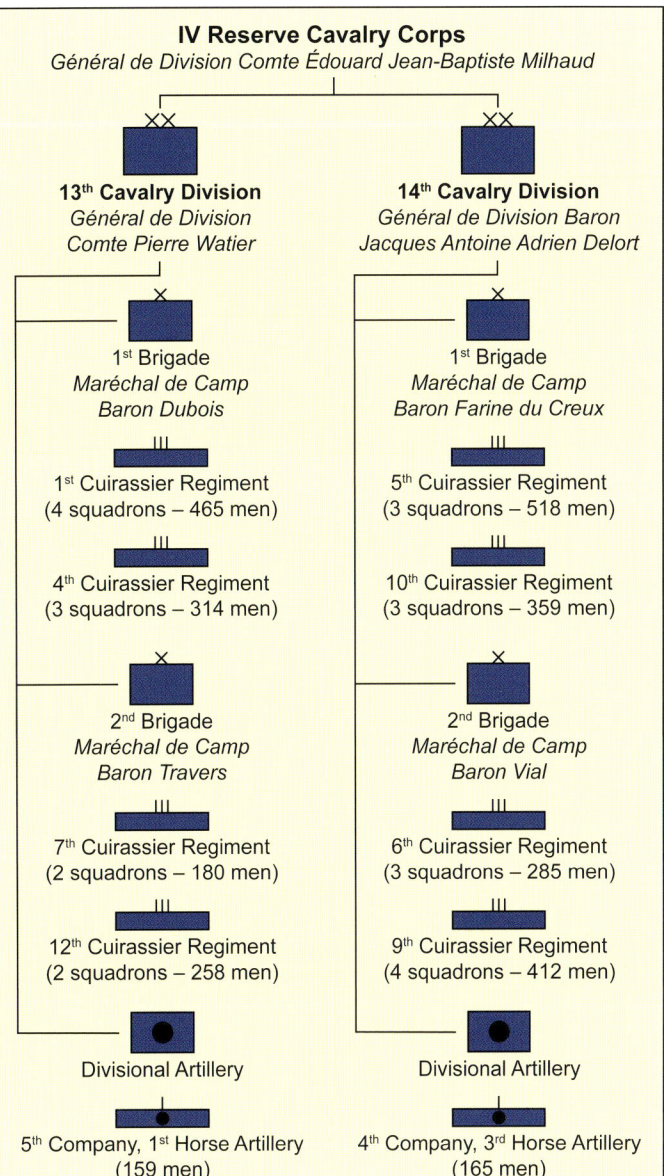

Organization and uniforms of the French Northern Army in June 1815

The French troops had little time to mobilize for the fight against the Allies under Wellington and Blücher. For this reason, it must be assumed that some of the troops were insufficiently supplied with uniforms and equipment. In the following description, as well as in the plate texts, we have therefore oriented ourselves to the possible appearance in June 1815.

General Staff

In contrast to Wellington or Blücher, Napoleon led an extensive general staff, which was based on the basic structures of the staff organization established in the Napoleonic Wars. Two areas were distinguished, namely the *"Maison Militaire"*, which was directly subordinate to Napoleon, and the actual general staff, the *"Etat-Major Général"*.

Maison Militaire

In addition to Napoleon's personal aide-de-camp, the Grand Marshal of the Palace, Général de Division Comte Henri-Gatien Bertrand, this section included general and staff officers who were directly subordinate to Napoleon and were entrusted by him with special tasks.

One should first of all mention the emperor's aides-de-camp, all of whom were generals during the 1815 campaign. These adjutants were selected on the basis of Napoleon's personal trust and, above all, their experience in previous campaigns. This was because they were to perform select tasks, sometimes with responsibility over troops, in special situations during campaigns or battles. In 1815, this select circle included the *Généraux de Division* Corbineau, Dejean, Drouot, Flahaut de la Billarderie and Lebrun, as well as the *Maréchaux de Camp* de la Bédoyère, Bernard and Bussy. Each of these generals had a few adjutants (aides de camp) at his personal disposal.

Another important part of the *Maison Militaire* were the twelve personal orderlies (*officiers d'ordonnance*), also known as Napoleon's "eyes and ears". They were entrusted by him with reconnaissance and the delivery of important orders and were therefore expected to have a sufficient number of horses ready for their use. The most famous orderly officer was Colonel Gourgaud, who also wrote an account of the campaign of 1815; besides him, only officers of the rank of captain were employed among the orderlies.

Etat-Major Général

The actual general staff of the army was headed by the *Major Général*. This post was held for many years by *Maréchal* Berthier, but during the 1815 campaign it was filled by *Maréchal* Jean de Dieu Soult. He was assisted by the *Général de Division* Comte Bailly de Monthion, who in turn was assisted by the three *Maréchaux de Camp* Couture, Gressot and Lebel.

The general staff also included experienced officers with the functions as adjutant-commandant as well as adjutants and *adjoints à l'état-major général*. In the 1815 campaign, five officers were entrusted with the function of adjutant-commandant, all with the rank of colonel. Adjutants and *adjoints* included six colonels, two *majors* (lieutenant colonel equivalents), 15 *chefs de battalion* (major equivalents) ten *capitaines*, and one *sous-lieutenant* (second lieutenant).

In addition, smaller staffs existed for the special troops, especially for the artillery, the park (*train*), the engineers (*génie*) and the administration. The Topographical Bureau, which was responsible for providing maps, should also be mentioned.

Uniforms of the General Staff

First, we will describe the general officers' uniforms, which were prescribed for the ranks of *Maréchal d'Empire*, *Général de Division* and *Maréchal de Camp*. The *Maréchal de Camp* corresponds to the former *Général de Brigade* and dates back to the renaming of the old title by Louis XVIII in 1814.

The **uniforms of the marshals (*maréchaux*) and generals (*généraux*)** changed little since the 1803 decrees, and in the field consisted of a single-breasted dark blue frock coat (*frac*) with gold buttons and gold decorative braid on the collar, cuffs, and around the waist buttons, which varied according to rank. The coat-tails were blue with gold emblems (eagle wings with lightning bolts). They were accompanied by white pants tucked into black riding boots. A gold-colored sash was placed around the waist, which had inlaid colored sections, namely white for a *maréchal*, red for a *général de division*, and light blue for a *maréchal de camp*. The gold epaulettes with thick "bouillon" fringes displayed crossed marshal's staffs for a *maréchal*, and three stars for a *général de division* and two stars for a *maréchal de camp*). They also wore a black bicorne hat with cockade and white (*maréchal* and commanding *général de division*) or black (generals - *généraux*) feather trim along the edge. A saber in a gilded iron scabbard was worn on red, gold-tipped drag straps on the waistbelt. For the *maréchal de camp*, the straps were sky blue with gold piping. Saddlecloths and pistol holster covers were made of crimson velour with gold trim that varied according to rank, and the leather gear was black with gilded metal parts.

The uniforms of *adjutants-commandants* or *adjoints à l'état-major* in 1815 was also still based on the decrees of September 1803. In the field, they wore the undress uniform consisting of a single-breasted dark blue coat with gilded buttons, white or dark blue pants, black leather boots, and a black bicorne hat without feather decoration. The coat had gold braid on the collar, cuffs and waist buttons, and gold epaulettes with thick fringes. The *adjudant-commander* was distinguished by the number of braids, namely three on the cuffs and around the waist buttons, while the *adjoints* had only two. Both ranks had two braids on each side of the collar. The saber, in a black leather scabbard with gilded reinforcements, hung from black leather waistbelt and suspending straps with gold edging, the rectangular belt buckle was gilded. The dark blue saddle cloths and holster covers had gold trim and were accompanied by black bridles.

The **Aides de Camp** wore the undress uniform in the field, consisting of dark blue, single-breasted coat with gilt buttons and sky-blue cuffs, turnbacks and collar. This was accompanied by dark blue pants worn in black leather boots and the black bicorne hat without feather decoration. The rank was distinguished with the epaulettes according to the appropriate regulation, and in addition, to mark the duty assignment, there was an armband with golden braids and fringes. This armband was white for aides de camp of a *maréchal*, red for that of a *général de division* and sky blue for that of a *maréchal de camp*. The armament and horse furniture were as for *adjutants-commandants* and *adjoints*. A regulation of 1812 required the replacement of the sky-blue collars and cuffs with ones of pale yellow. The extent to which this regulation was implemented cannot be determined. Whether the fancy uniforms of the aides de camp from earlier times in the Napoleonic Wars, some of which deviated significantly from the regulations, were also worn in 1815 is rather unlikely. Even for these officers, the time to procure their individual uniforms and equipment was very short, which rather speaks for the described, simpler uniform.

However, the uniform of the Emperor's **Officiers d'Ordonnance** was different from that of the aides de camp. It consisted of a medium blue coat with pointed lapels and silver-plated buttons. Silver-colored decorative braids were attached to the collar, pointed cuffs, and around the waist buttons, plus they were piped in silver. A silver-colored epaulet was worn on the left shoulder according to rank, and silver-colored aiguilettes were attached to the right shoulder. A red vest with silver lacing and edging was worn under the coat. The pants were of the same color as the coat with silver decorations, and black hussar-style boots were also worn. The shako, which was actually prescribed, was replaced in the field by a black bicorne hat.

Imperial Guard Troops

In addition to the formation or reorganization of the Bourbon line units, Napoleon also tackled the reorganization of his tactical reserve - the Imperial Guard - after his return from Elba. Although the short time between April and the march to the theater of operations in June 1815 posed enormous challenges in providing uniforms, equipment and armaments, the Guard could at least draw on a core of experienced soldiers and cadres who were already equipped. Thus, three divisions of infantry were formed, namely a Grenadier Division, a Chasseur Division and a Young Guard Division. The Guards Cavalry was divided into one division of Light Cavalry and one division of Heavy Cavalry. In addition, there were the artillery, the train, the engineers (*génie*) and some companies of marines.

The infantry regiments included two battalions of four companies each; each infantry company was to include one captain, one lieutenant, two *sous-lieutenants*, one *sergent-major*, six *sergents*, twelve *caporaux*, one *fourrier*, two drummers, and 174 soldiers in case of war. All cavalry regiments were to include four squadrons of two companies each. The wartime strength of the companies was set at 150 men.

For artillery, six foot companies and four mounted companies were raised in 1815. One company served one battery. The authorized number for each company of foot artillery was: two *capitaines*, one lieutenant, two *sous-lieutenants*, one *sergent-major*, four *sergents*, eight *caporaux*, one *fourrier*, two drummers, 32 first-class gunners, and 64 second-class gunners. Each mounted company included two *capitaines*, one lieutenant, one *sous-lieutenant*, one *sergeant-major*, four *sergents*, six *caporaux*, one *fourrier*, three trumpeters, 25 first-class cannoneers, and 50 second-class cannoneers. In addition, there were four craftsmen for all companies, including two armorers and, for the mounted companies, two farriers. The mounted companies had six 6-pounder guns each. For the foot companies, two batteries of eight 6-pounder guns each and four batteries of eight 12-pounder guns each were formed. These batteries were all assigned to the Old Guard; for the Young Guard, only batteries of the line could be attached for the campaign.

Grenadier Corps of the Imperial Guard

The *Corps royal des Grenadiers de France*, formed under the Bourbons on July 1, 1814, also from parts of the disbanded Imperial Guard, was disbanded on April 8, 1815, and transformed into three **regiments of Guard grenadiers (*Grenadiers à Pied de la Garde*).** The first regiment also included the soldiers of the Guard Battalion who had returned from the Isle of Elba. Shortly thereafter, a fourth regiment of Guards was formed, but only one battalion participated in the campaign.

The headgear of the four grenadier regiments consisted primarily of the black bearskin cap, which is also verified for the Imperial Guard attack according to reports from British participants of the campaign. In addition, the grenadiers were also supposed to have a bicorne hat and a forage, which, however, were available in insufficient numbers for all four regiments in June. The bearskin cap had a brass cap plate with an embossed eagle and a red cap top with a white grenade on it. There is also evidence that bearskin caps were fitted with a black leather cap top instead of the red cap top. According to reports, at least the 1st Regiment may have been equipped with a sufficient number of bicorne hats. In case the bicorne hat was worn, the bearskin cap, if available, was tucked into a blue and white striped cover that could be strapped onto the knapsack.

For uniforms, the grenadiers could have reverted back to a coat and a dark blue greatcoat, both of which were in sufficient supply in 1815. The dark blue coat had brass buttons, white lapels, red straight cuffs, and red long lapels that ended flush with the turnbacks. The turnbacks were decorated with orange grenades on a yellow background. The cuffs had white serrated flaps that closed with three brass buttons. Red epaulettes were worn on both shoulders, and insignia indicating the rank and time served were sewn onto the sleeves.

Due to the rainy weather, it is not improbable that the Guard Grenadiers were wearing their greatcoats at Waterloo, which is also reported by an officer who participated in the events of June 18, 1815. The prescribed coat with a stand-up collar was fastened with two rows of brass buttons. However, a single-breasted model is also described, which had wide red square-cut braids with buttons attached on each side of the collar, as well as red piping on the cuffs. It is believed that both models were worn in the 1815 campaign.

As pants, besides the common tight white breeches, which were tucked into dark gray or black gaiters, long pants made of blue fabric are also shown. However, even taking into account the soldiers of the Elba battalion who were incorporated, their number was still too small to equip the entire 1st Regiment with them as intended. Long white pants are also described, but they did not comply with regulations.

The 4th Regiment of Guard Grenadiers may have been the most difficult to equip, as it had to be newly formed and marched from Paris toward the Northern Army partly wearing overcoats and dress coats. Some of the soldiers wore older bearskin caps, some bicorne hats, so that according to an eyewitness no twenty soldiers of a company had the same appearance.

As equipment, the guard grenadiers carried a black cartridge box with a brass eagle in the center of the lid and four small brass grenades in the corners. It was worn on a wide whitened leather bandolier over the left shoulder. Different covers made of cloth existed to protect the cartridge box. The backpack, made of calfskin, was carried with straps, also whitened, over the crossed bandoliers. A second bandolier, which passed over the right shoulder to the left hip, supported the short saber in a black leather scabbard. The bayonet could be attached next to the sword's scabbard. The musket was mostly of the model 1777, some grenadiers could also be equipped with the musket M1777 *corrigé an IX (de la Garde)*.[2]

Officers in the field probably wore a dark blue single-breasted coat with dark blue collars and cuffs, red turnbacks, and gilded buttons. As insignia they wore the golden epaulettes according to their rank and a gilded gorget. Their pants were white and tucked into black boots with brown cuffs. Blue loose-fitting pants are also reported for officers (at least of the 1st Regiment). Headgear for this uniform consisted of a black bicorne hat with a cockade attached with gold strips. The rolled up dark blue greatcoat could be worn over the (left) shoulder.

Drummers and pipers wore the grenadier's uniform and had the NCO's scarlet epaulettes with gold stripes on the slide as a decoration.

By imperial decree of April 8, 1815, eight **Tirailleur regiments** were to be raised, each of two battalions of four companies. They were to be formed from volunteers and mainly re-conscripted former soldiers of the Young Guard, but soldiers of the line were also enrolled. Due to slow recruitment, only the first six regiments were formed and a level of 120 men per company was set by Napoleon on June 5. Only when a regiment thus reached a target strength of 960 men were the companies to be successively increased to 150 men. The Order of Battle shows that only the 1st Tirailleur Regiment reached a strength of over 1,100 men.

Their uniform consisted of a simple black shako with brass eagle as the guard emblem and red pompom over the cockade. The coat was dark blue and in the so-called "Bardin cut" with short coattails and straight lapels. The collar as well as the pointed cuffs were scarlet. While the collar was piped dark blue, the lapels and cuffs had white piping. The red turnbacks were decorated with white eagles. In 1815, the cloth epaulets worn until 1814 were not reintroduced and red epaulets were prescribed instead. The white pants were tucked into black gaiters that were cut out in the front similar to hussar boots.

Noncommissioned officers had gold eagles on their turnbacks in addition to the rank chevrons on their sleeves. Officers wore the uniform of the former tirailleurs-grenadiers, which prescribed a uniform of the Guard grenadiers, but with a shako whose upper and lower edges were edged with black velour. It is unlikely whether the earlier prescribed gold trim and applied gold-colored stars on the

---

2   Model 1777 corrected in the year 1800, or IX in the French Revolutionary Calendar.

upper velour band were still worn in 1815. Until the old regiments were disbanded in 1814, drummers had gold trim along the lapels, collar, and cuffs. Again, it does not appear that this uniform was still worn in the 1815 campaign.

Chasseurs (à Pied) Corps of the Imperial Guard

In parallel with the Guard Grenadiers, four **regiments of *Chasseurs à Pied*** (literally 'hunters on foot) were also formed by decree of April 8, 1815, also with the same structure as their comrades of the Grenadiers. They were formed from the *Corps royal des Chasseurs à pied de France*, from the two companies that returned from Elba, from soldiers of line regiments and finally from (re)enlisted former soldiers. In this process, the two companies from Elba and the most experienced soldiers from the Royal Chasseur Corps were to be formed into the 1st Regiment. Based on this decision the target strength was quickly reached. The other soldiers of the disbanded corps as well as soldiers of the line were incorporated into the 2nd Regiment - this, together with the 1st Chasseurs à Pied Regiment, formed the Chasseur Corps of the Old Guard. The forming of the 3rd and 4th Regiments of the Middle Guard could not be completed until the end of May 1815.

The extent of the distribution of uniforms and equipment for the chasseurs à pied can be concluded based on the 2nd Regiment's preserved book of orders. Thus, the first two regiments were fully equipped at the beginning of June, the 3rd Regiment was not fully equipped, while the 4th Regiment could only with difficulty field an equipped battalion. Since the two regiments of the Middle Guard had already marched to the Northern Army on June 5, it remains unclear how they could have been fully equipped by the time they entered the campaign. One must assume that, at least in the case of the 4th Regiment, differing equipment characterized the appearance of the personnel..

The black bearskin cap without a cap plate and cap cover was available in sufficient numbers in Belgium until the first battles, so that the soldiers of all four regiments were equipped with that headgear. Also the green plumes with red tip, actually intended for the dress uniform, were available in large numbers and were probably worn at the Battle of Waterloo.

The situation was much worse with the bicorne hats, which were probably only available to the two regiments of the Old Guard, but not in sufficient numbers for all the men mobilized. However, forage caps could again be issued to all soldiers of the regiments.

The coats with long coattails could also be distributed to the deployed regiments in their entirety. Some of them still dated from 1814 but had not yet exceeded their prescribed period of wear. The dark blue coat had red pointed cuffs that were piped with white. The white lapels were cut high above the white vest. Brass buttons and red epaulettes with green sliders complemented the coat. The red turnbacks featured an orange horn on the outside and a grenade on the inside, both symbols on a white background. The NCOs' rank and time served insignia were attached to the sleeves.

The regiments of the Middle Guard may have initially worn tight white pants, which were tucked into black gaiters, or long white trousers. In the 1st and 2nd Regiments (Old Guard), long blue trousers were more common, but variations may have occurred here as well. Later, the soldiers of the two regiments of the Middle Guard may also have received blue pants, at least partially.

Overcoats were available in sufficient numbers or were produced before the start of hostilities, so that the chasseurs, unlike the grenadiers, also went to war with greatcoats. The model complied with the regulation by having two rows of brass buttons and red patches on the collar and cuffs.

The cartridge boxes, decorated with a brass eagle and brass grenades and brass horns on the lids, could be delivered to the troops of the four chasseur regiments in time for the battles of June 16. The knapsack, leather gear, and sidearm were the same as those used by the Guard Grenadiers.

Officers were ordered to wear a dark blue single-breasted coat with red turnbacks and gilt buttons with decorations on the turnbacks. Long white trousers were to be worn with it.

Drummers, unlike their fellow grenadiers, were clearly distinguished, namely with scarlet swallow's nests under their epaulettes. The collar, cuffs and the swallow's nests were trimmed with gold braid.

Regiments were also raised for the Young Guard in the Chasseur Corps, namely the **voltigeur regiments** by decree of April 8, 1815. A total of eight regiments were raised, although the 7th and 8th regiments, which were decreed last on May 12, achieved only a small fighting strength. In particular, the 1st Regiment, formed with, among others, the Flanker Battalion (*Bataillon de Flanqueurs*) returning from Elba, reached its target strength of 1,200 men. For the 3rd Regiment, which was also moving toward the Northern Army's fighting, not even 1,000 men could be mobilized, and the 2nd Regiment, also intended for the Northern Army, did not march north until June 18. The 1st Regiment can be considered a worthy Guard unit in the Young Guard because of its strength and its almost complete team of experienced soldiers - for in addition to the aforementioned Flanker Battalion, the former Elba Chasseurs, numerous Corsican recruits and officers of the 35th Light Infantry Regiment and NCOs of the 3rd Foreign Battalion (*Bataillon Étranger*) joined the regiment.

The first three regiments of Voltigeurs are likely to have been almost completely equipped with the prescribed items but short sabers can be completely confirmed only for the 1st Regiment.

The headgear consisted of a simple shako with a brass eagle emblem and a green pompom over the cockade. Many Voltigeurs may have protected the shako with a black cover. The dark blue coat of the "Bardin" cut (*habit-veste*) had brass buttons, a yellow collar with a blue piping, and pointed red cuffs that were piped in white. On the red turnbacks, which were piped in white, were orange hunting horns on a white background. The green epaulettes had yellow crescents; only the 2nd Regiment was issued blue epaulettes with yellow piping. Greatcoats were also issued, known to be beige-gray for the troops.

The wide pants were white and worn over the dark gray or black gaiters. The black cartridge box was worn on a white bandolier over the left shoulder, the cartridge box lid was decorated with a brass horn. If the soldier did not have a short saber, such as in the 3rd Regiment, the bayonet scabbard was attached to the bandolier. Officers are likely to have gone to the field in a single-breasted coat with a yellow collar piped with blue. Only the turnbacks were red. Gold epaulettes according to rank and a gold gorget were worn as rank insignia. Pants were dark blue and worn over the boots. If the men brought overcoats, they were worn rolled up over the shoulder. The simple black bicorne hat had a green pompom above the cockade. Drummers are likely to have resembled troops like was the case for the tirailleurs; the earlier gold braids were probably no longer supplied.

Marines of the Imperial Guard

With the new formation of the Guard in April 1815, a unit (*équipage*) of marines was also raised, to a target strength of 150 men. They were placed under the command of *Général de Division* Haxo, commander of the engineer (*genie*) units in the Imperial Guard.

The state of the uniforms after the unit's formation can only be insufficiently reconstructed. On June 6, 1815, the delivery of overcoats, gaiters, shoes and forage caps to the sailors has been confirmed. A report of June 9, 1815, mentions the departure of 62 sailors and two officers, who were probably fully uniformed and equipped the day before. Sailors sent later were to be equipped en route.

The distinctive uniform piece of the dress uniform was a blue "*paletot*" without coattails with orange lacing and brass buttons. The collar was blue, the pointed cuffs scarlet. The collar and cuffs were edged with orange braid. This *paletot* was accompanied by blue trousers with orange braid trim on the outsides and as Hungarian knots on the thighs. The shako was decorated with orange braid on the top and bottom and orange cording. The leather gear was black, along with a naval saber in a black leather scabbard with brass reinforcements. Brass anchors were on the cartridge box covers and associated bandolier as decoration. The saber bandolier, worn over the right shoulder, had a brass buckle with an embossed anchor. However, because of the problems in equipment mentioned above, the marines are more likely to have marched into the 1815 campaign in dark blue overcoats with two rows of brass buttons as well as dark blue wide pants. The shako was probably worn with a black cover due to the rainy weather. As an alternative to the coat, until their disbandment in 1814. marines were also allowed a simple Spencer with two rows of brass buttons, pointed blue cuffs, and open blue collar. The collar and cuffs were trimmed in orange, and the shoulders were covered with yellow metal scales. Whether this coat was also delivered in 1815 cannot be determined. The pants in the field were probably plain dark blue without braid trim.

NCOs wore rank insignia like those of the Guards Cavalry. Officers in 1815 might have been dressed in a single-breasted dark blue coat with gold-edged cuffs and collars. They wore a black bicorne hat and dark blue pants tucked into black hussar boots.

Imperial Guard Cavalry

The Guard cavalry was divided into the light units, the *Chasseurs à Cheval* (literally 'hunters on horses') and the two regiments of *chevau-légers lanciers* (light horse lancers), and the heavy units, consisting of the horse grenadiers (*grenadiers à cheval*), the dragoons and the elite gendarmerie.

The **Chasseurs à Cheval** were formed by the decree of April 8, 1815, from the *Corps royal des Chasseurs à cheval de France*, which was formed from the former Guard C*hasseurs à Cheval* after Napoleon's abdication in 1814. A decree of May 15 also ordered the formation of a regiment for the Young Guard, but this could not be implemented in time for the operations in Belgium.

Due to the continued existence of the former Guard Chasseurs in the Bourbon army, the *Chasseurs à Cheval* of 1815 were able to draw on sufficient existing uniform items and equipment. Thus, they strongly resembled the appearance of this famous Guard regiment from 1813 to 1814.

The black busby (colpak) was worn without the feather plume, which remained in the depot. The busby's red cap bag may also have been discarded. The green dolman had orange lacing, brass buttons, pointed red cuffs, and orange piping on the collar, cuffs, and seams. The red pelisses were most likely not worn in the field by the troopers. Green overalls with black leather lining and red trim on the outer seams were worn instead of the tight breeches. The barrel sash consisted of green cords pulled through red wool loops. The sabretaches, formerly covered with embroidered cloth, were replaced by plain black leather sabretaches with a brass eagle as an emblem. The saber and sabretache were fixed to a white waist belt. Over the left shoulder hung the white bandolier with the cartridge pouch. The cartridge pouch was supposed to display a brass horn with eagle, however, at Waterloo the lids may have been seen with horn only, as there was no longer time to produce the eagles in place of the removed fleur-de-lis badges. The green shabraque and green valise had a wide orange border with a red outer edging.

Officers wore the same uniform, possibly taking pelisses with them on campaign. Their buttons, piping and cording were gold, their rank insignia were gold chevrons above the cuffs. Trumpeters were to wear a blue dolman and blue pants of the same cut as the enlisted men, but with a red collar. However, this cannot be definitively confirmed, so trumpeters may also have been attired in green dolman.

With the **Chevau-Légers Lanciers,** Napoleon continued the tradition of the earlier regiments, namely by creating a *Lanciers polonais* (Polish Lancers) and *Lanciers rouges* (Red Lancers) similar in appearance to the 1st (Polish) and 2nd (Dutch or Red) Lancers that had existed until 1814. The first squadron of the regiment, newly formed in 1815, was formed from the Polish Lancers who returned from Elba with Napoleon, as well as some more former Polish soldiers living in France. The other four squadrons were formed from the *Corps royal des chevau-légers lanciers de*

France, into which the old Guard Lanciers had been transferred in 1814. Each of the five squadrons was to be comprised of two companies, while the first (Polish) squadron went to the field with only one combined company totaling 115 men.

When it came to the uniform of the Polish Lancers, the decree of April 22, 1815, stipulated that they should be equipped with the old uniform prescribed until 1814. However, the common description in British memoirs that the Polish Lancers attacked in parade uniform may be doubted in view of the practice prevailing in the other units. For a further description, see the captions of Lyall's two plates.

The *Lanciers Rouges* probably wore the old simple field uniform, i.e., the *czapka* without the cording and plume, but with a black wax cover. Their *kurtka* coat was scarlet with dark blue lapels, collar and pointed cuffs. A dark blue trim was placed along the seams at the back and the back of the sleeves. There was a yellow retaining cord on the left shoulder, and a yellow epaulet with a dark blue crescent on the right. The lapels were probably worn folded over one another so that only the dark blue piping could be seen. The pants were replaced in the field by dark blue overalls with black leather trim and scarlet stripes on the outer seams. There were brass buttons on the side stripes. The shabraques were dark blue and had yellow trim; it is no longer possible to reconstruct whether the decoration with a yellow, crowned "N" in the rear corners was actually attached. More about the uniforms, especially those of the officers and trumpeters, is discussed in the captions on Lyall's plates.

The Empress' Dragoons were also formed from an existing body of troops. This was because the old Guards Dragoon Regiment continued as the *Corps royal des Dragons de France in* 1814 after Napoleon's abdication. The decree of April 8, 1815, then led to its being renamed to the old designation.

The uniform consisted of the old familiar coat with brass buttons, white lapels, green collar, red turnbacks, and straight red cuffs with white cuff flaps. The turnbacks had orange grenades. There was an orange contra-epaulet without fringe on both shoulders, with additional retaining cords on the right shoulder. The gray cloth pants were tucked into heavy cavalry boots. The old helmet with black horsehair tail and red feather plume served as headgear. Whether the plume was also worn on the campaign cannot be proven. The dragoon's straight sabre was attached to the white waist belt, which was closed with a brass buckle. The black cartridge pouch hung from the white leather bandolier. The shabraque, pistol holster covers and valise were green with orange trim. There was an orange crown in the back corners of the shabraque.

What was special about the uniform of the non-commissioned officers (NCOs) was that the majority of them went on the campaign with the single-breasted surtout. This had green cuffs without flaps, only the turnbacks remained red. In addition, they had the rank insignia and scarlet-gold retaining cords. For the officers' and buglers' uniforms, please refer to the captions in the plates.

Like the dragoons, the old **Grenadiers à Cheval** (Horse Grenadiers) were taken over by Louis XVIII and transferred to the *Corps royal des Cuirassiers de France.* By the decree of April 8, 1815, the unit was again given its old name. In their outfitting with uniforms, an attempt was made to regain the old appearance from the years before Napoleon's abdication, which was also achieved by making numerous modifications. Thus the Horse Grenadiers went to the campaign with a bearskin cap without cording and a feather plume. On the top of the cap was a red patch with an orange cross. The cap was held in place by brass chin scales. However, unlike many depictions of a surtout, the Horse Grenadiers were equipped with a dark blue coat with white lapels, brass buttons, and straight red cuffs with white cuff flaps. The red turnbacks displayed orange grenades and the epaulettes were orange. Like the dragoons, the Horse Grenadiers went to the field on horseback wearing gray cloth trousers. The straight sabre with grenade emblem in the basket was attached to a white waistbelt. The black cartridge pouch was suspended by a white bandolier that passed over the left shoulder. Its lid had a diamond-shaped brass plate embossed with three stars and a coat of arms. The shabraque, pistol holster covers and valise were dark blue with orange trim, and the back corners had an orange crown or grenade.

Officers may have worn the same uniform, only with gilded buttons, epaulettes and retaining cords on the coat. Again, the surtout seems unlikely. Trumpeters probably had sky blue coats of the same cut as the enlisted men, but with crimson collars, lapels, and cuffs, all of which had gold trim around the edges. Their epaulettes and retaining cords were mixed crimson and gold. Their caps had a crimson patch on top with a white cross. Their shabraques, pistol holster covers and valises were crimson instead of dark blue.

An elite gendarme company (**Gendarmerie d'Élite**) was also re-established with the decree to reconstitute the Imperial Guard. It was to be recruited from former members of the former unit as well as recommendations of the Inspector General for the Gendarmerie. A squadron of two companies was to be formed, but at Waterloo there were only 106 men at company strength. The coat was similar in cut to those of the Horse Grenadiers, but with white metallic buttons and scarlet lapels, turnbacks, and cuffs that had dark blue cuff flaps. The turnbacks had white grenades as emblems. The white retaining cords were worn on the left shoulder, unlike the other Guard units. A dark blue single-breasted surtout might have been worn instead of the coat. The vest and trousers were yellowish brown according to Gendarmerie tradition, though gray pants are also cited for the field uniform. Although bearskin caps were commissioned, it is quite possible that the gendarmes still went to the field wearing the iron helmets of the old *Gendarmes de la Chasse.* These had a brass comb and plate, with a black *chenille* crest on the comb. The cartridge pouch bandoliers and waistbelts were yellowish brown and had white edging. The shabraques, pistol holster covers and valises were dark blue, like those of the Guard Horse Grenadiers, but had white borders and trim.

Officers had a similar outfit, except that the coat or surtout was trimmed with silver buttons, epaulettes, and retaining cords. Trumpeters may have had a surtout with white trim on the collar and cuffs.

Imperial Guard Artillery

The decree of April 8, 1815, ordered the formation of ten batteries, four of them mounted, all of them assigned to the Old Guard. For the formation, former Guard artillerymen were to be recruited, if possible, but soldiers for the line were also integrated into the newly formed batteries.

When the uniforms were procured, the ten companies could not be supplied with uniforms and equipment at the same time; some items such as coats could not be delivered in full.

The **foot artillery (*artillerie à pied*)** had the uniform of the Guard artillerymen disbanded in 1814. This consisted of a black fur cap with a visor, red cording and a red plume. The cording and plume may have been removed due to the rainy weather at Waterloo. In addition to the bearskin cap, the artillerymen also possessed a dark blue forage cap with red trim and piping. The coat and pants were dark blue. On the coat, only turnbacks, probably without emblems, and straight cuffs were trimmed in scarlet, with additional red piping on the lapels, collar, and coattail pockets. The epaulettes were red and the buttons were brass. The trousers were worn over the black gaiters. The soldiers, who had not received a coat by the time of the battles, may have worn a dark blue overcoat fastened with a row of brass buttons. This may have had red piping on the collar and cuffs. In addition to short sabers and bayonets, the artillerymen also carried a black cartridge pouch on which was a brass eagle above crossed cannon barrels.

The officers' uniform may have been worn as depicted by Charles Lyall on the plate on the 1815 campaign, but a single-breasted dark blue coat with red turnbacks and a red piped collar was also common for the field uniform.

In the case of the drummers, it may be that in 1815 their coats also had the designated red lapels and gold trim on the lapels, collar, and cuffs.

The horse artillery could also be largely equipped with their characteristic uniform items until the first battles in June 1815. This consisted of a short black fur cap, the busby with a red cap bag, but without the cording and plume, which were left at the depot. The dark blue coat had brass buttons, pointed red cuffs, and red piping on the lapels and collar. The red turnbacks displayed blue grenade emblems. The so-called "*trèfle*" (trefoil) epaulette was fastened on the right shoulder, and red aiguillettes hung from the left shoulder. Under the pointed lapels the dark blue vest was visible. This was trimmed with red piping and frogging. The pants were dark blue, reinforced with black leather on the inside and bottom, and had red trim on the outsides, trimmed with brass buttons. As protection against the weather, the artillerymen could put on a dark blue riding overcoat. Over the left shoulder they wore the white cartridge pouch bandolier, to which the black cartridge pouch was attached. The saber with brass scabbard hung from two white drag straps. Sabretaches were no longer made for the artillerymen in 1815. The dark blue shabraque had a red border as well as red grenades in the pointed rear corners. The dark blue valise had red border trim on the sides.

For officers, the busby could be decorated with gold cording, a red cap bag and a red plume. The coat was the same as that of the enlisted men, only with gilded aiguillettes and epaulettes according to rank. The dark blue pants were decorated with gold rank braid on the thighs and were tucked into black Hungarian boots. The richly decorated cartridge pouch bandolier was likely worn in the field with a red cover with gilt buttons. Gold braid was applied to the red trim of their shabraques and valises.

Trumpeters had lighter coats and pants of the same cut as the enlisted men, but the cuffs and collar were blue. The collar, lapels and cuffs were trimmed with gold braid.

Génie (Engineers) of the Imperial Guard

When the Imperial Guard was formed on April 8, 1815, a company of engineer sappers (*Sappeurs des Génie*) was also formed, which was to consist of a squad of sappers (*mineurs*). These *mineurs* were to be recruited from former Sappers of the Guard. In addition, *Sappeur-Mineurs* were to be incorporated from volunteers from the line engineer (*génie*) units. The target strength was set at 200 men in case of war.

For the uniforms, it was not possible to fall back on old stocks of the former uniforms, but these had to be newly manufactured. Their appearance was supposed to be oriented on the uniforms of the former *Garde-Sappeurs*. Since Charles Lyall's plate comes close to that appearance, a detailed description is omitted here.

Line Units

With the Bourbon royal takeover of power in May 1814 (the 1st Restoration), the former - too large - imperial army was also reorganized. The army structure was essentially retained, but regiments were disbanded in all branches of the armed forces and the number of men was reduced.

On his return, Napoleon retained the regimental numbers, but cut the battalion numbers and reinforced the companies with the freed-up men. In addition, the ranks were replenished with new recruits. Additionally he reinstated the old numbers to the units. Overall, however, there was a shortage of equipment and horses, which numerous measures only partially remedied.

Uniforms in general

For the line units, the so-called Bardin Instructions, the first comprehensive regulation since the Revolution, were in effect since 1812, which newly regulated the clothing, the cut and partly the insignia. The main goal was to standardize and simplify the uniform. It was implemented slowly, also due to the events of the war, only gradually carried out in 1813–1814 and was associated with subsequent modifications.

During the Restoration, the specifications and existing devices were largely retained, but the imperial symbols were exchanged for the royal Bourbon ones, such as the fleur-de-lis emblems and the white cockade.

The shako, model 1812, was used unchanged and for the center companies was only fitted with a pompom showing the company by means of its color. The grenadiers had a red pompom with a red braid trim around the body. The Voltigeurs had the same arrangement only in yellow. The shako plate, established by Bardin, was reused after the return, it was semicircular at the bottom with the number placed below the eagle. During the royal period the eagle emblem was removed, so that in the 1815 campaign often only the lower shield was visible. Usually, the shako was covered with gray or brown linen or black oil wax cloth for protection.

The coat (*habit veste*) had lapels closed to the waist, which were white as the basic color for the line and the blue in the coat color for the light infantry. The same cut was used by the cavalry and technical branches such as chasseurs, chevaulegers, dragoons and artillery. Here, too, the lapels were in the distinction or coat color with different piping colors.

Pants were tightly cut to match the dress uniform, but the gaiters were shortened to below the knee. The cavalry also wore tight pants and, depending on the type, tall cuffed boots or short Hungarian-cut boots.

Drummers and Trumpeters

During the imperial period, these were usually distinguished from the enlisted men by their occasionally striking colors of red, yellow, light blue or green. Napoleon tried to counteract this diversity and also fancy designs by a uniform model, which was only partially successful up to 1814. The so-called "imperial *livree*" was of green cloth and richly trimmed with yellow braid. The braid was embroidered with eagle emblems and the "N". The cut could be single-breasted or with lapels in white or red.

With the Restoration in 1814, the royal *livree* was introduced in blue with a white lace and fleur-de-lis pattern. After Napoleon's return, attempts were quickly made either to obtain the imperial *livree* or the fabric for it, or to rework the royal *livree*. Thus, some of the royal emblems were removed, but the laces were retained or replaced with simple white ribbons. In the case of the green *livree*, only yellow laces and stripes were used when available, or omitted completely.

However, non-standard types of coats were also worn (e.g., by the 1st and 19th Infantry Regiments), such as the blue coat with lapels that were framed with white and red braid and also had seven sleeve stripes each of the same braid.

The cavalry branches' shabraques had two basic patterns, for example, the heavy cavalry used white sheepskins with lace edging, to which a rectangular cloth was attached. The color and lace varied by branch and regiment. The light cavalry and the horse artillery also used sheepskin as a saddle blanket, but without a cloth. The trumpeters had as a distinction a black fleece with colored braid border.

The armament remained the same throughout the Revolution and the Imperial period, except for modifications. The standard musket was the Model 1777 (Charleville; Model XIII). A shorter variant for the dragoons and light cavalry was the Model IX to XIII musket or carbine (*Mousqueton Model IX to XIII*). In addition, especially in 1815, various pistol models were issued to cavalry regiments as their sole firearms. As cutting and thrusting weapons, the heavy units received the Model XIII straight saber and the light regiments, as well as a large part of the technical troops, the Model XI curved saber.

Infantry

Organization

The backbone and the strongest arm of the army was the infantry, which was divided into the line infantry and light infantry. The light infantry differed only minimally from the line infantry. The actual tasks of the light infantry, such as skirmishing, were performed by the voltigeur companies in the light and line Infantry regiments.

The infantry had been reorganized by the royal decree of May 1814 and reduced from 134 to 105 regiments. Of these, 90 had been designated as line infantry and 15 regiments as light infantry. Each regiment numbered three battalions of six companies each, two of which formed the elite companies (grenadiers and voltigeurs). Since there were more than 130 formations before, they were renumbered from 1 to 90. The unused numbers in between were deleted. This left Napoleon with about 83,700 infantrymen in 1815.

Uniforms and equipment

In the spring of 1815, the implementation of standardization or regulation was limited. Besides the closed blue coat, the vest was also worn. It was single-breasted and made of white cloth without coattails and distinctions. Civilian clothes were also still worn under the overcoat. Since bad weather conditions prevailed during the first days of the campaign, the gray, beige or even the green overcoat was often worn. The long pants were usually the same color as the coats. However, striped pants or even the soldiers' own purchases in green, blue or brown were also worn. The center companies wore on a bandolier with cartridge pouch, on which was also the bayonet scabbard. The NCOs and the elite companies additionally had the short saber on a bandolier. In addition, they had the calfskin leather knapsack strapped to their backs. Linen sacks, haversacks, pots and field flasks completed the equipment.

Officers: In addition to the single-breasted surtout, dark blue short or long overcoats were used. In the field, gray and dark blue pants of various cuts were often worn. The rapier served as armament, and the saber for the grenadiers. As additional equipment, officers carried a brown leather shoulder bag for personal belongings. Instead of the shako, many officers preferred the bicorne hat made of black felt, which was usually kept simple and only featured the cockade.

Drummers: They wore *livrees* of various cuts and colors. The blue coat was complemented by braids sewn on the lapels, collars and sleeves.

Light infantry

Uniforms

The light infantry was generally dressed in the same cut as the line. What differed were the lapels, the cuffs and turnbacks which were dark blue. In addition, the cuffs were pointed. All facings were piped with white. The center companies - here chasseurs - had red collars and mostly shoulder straps in the coat color with white piping. In the elite companies, such as with the line, the carabiniers had red epaulettes, bands on the shako and plume or pompon. The Voltigeurs wore yellow collars, yellow or green epaulettes, and plumes or pompons. The long pants, like those of the line, were of different colors, in white, brown or blue, often with yellow piping.

For officers, the coats were cut like those of the enlisted men but with long coattails, but all the piping, rank insignia, gorget, and portepée were silver. In the field, officers often donned the single-breasted coat, which was made entirely of dark blue cloth except for the collar and wore long gray or blue pants with it.

For the drummers, there were no differences from the line regiments.

Swiss Regiment (*Regiment Suisse*)

Organization

Even though Napoleon tried to take over the Royal Swiss, which under the monarchy once again existed with four regiments, most of them refused to join the new service. By April 1815, only one battalion could be combined as a weak regiment under Colonel Stoffel. As the 2nd Regiment (in the sequence of the planned foreign regiment's numbering), it was the only one to fight in the campaign and took part under Marshal Grouchy in the fighting for the bridge crossings at Wavre on June 18. There it suffered such heavy losses and practically ceased to exist.

Uniform

It was uniformed like the line infantry, but the coat's basic color was red and the facings yellow. The uniform of the musicians is not documented.

Line Cavalry

Organization

Within this branch of arms, the French army distinguished between heavy cavalry, which included the cuirassiers, carabiniers, and dragoons, and light cavalry, such as hussars, chasseurs à cheval, and chevaulegers. In 1815, the regiments were organized from two to four squadrons of two companies each. In the Light, the 1st company of the 1st squadron was the elite unit and it was distinguished by its headgear or epaulettes.

Cuirassiers

The cuirassiers, like the carabiniers, were considered 'battle' cavalry and "shock weapons". Their task was to attack with massive force in order to break through or ride over enemy formations or lines.

Cuirassiers developed from the armored cavalry starting in the 17th century. Until the end of the First Empire, it made up 14 regiments, which were present at all the battlefields and carried out famous attacks even before Waterloo, such as at the Battle of Eylau in 1807 and at Borodino in 1812.

At the beginning of 1815 there were still twelve regiments, which had hardly changed in organization and uniform.

Uniforms and equipment

The iron, full cuirass and the bowl helmet with a horse tail were the typical appearance, which had hardly changed since the imperial times.

As with other troop units, there had been reductions and shortages of equipment here during the period of the first Restoration. Thus, the 11th Regiment had received only partial cuirasses. The straight saber was used as armament, and in the case of firearms, only the short carbine or a pistol hooked to the bandolier were used instead of muskets.

A plume was no longer worn on the helmet. The tight pants with cuffed boots were worn in different shades from gray to brown, often with leather inserts. In addition, long overalls without boots are also confirmed. The collet coats of the enlisted men were single-breasted and distinguished by the various distinctions on the collar, cuffs and turnbacks, which had a blue grenade emblem. The 1st Regiment wore, instead of the general red epaulettes, white epaulettes (former *Regiment du Roi*). The cuirass lining (cloth edgings on the cuirass) was red with white piping on the outsides.

The saddle cloths of white sheepskin with attached dark blue cloth corners were trimmed with a colored, jagged border.

The regiments that participated in the 1815 campaign had the following distinctions:

Regiment	Collar and Turnbacks	Cuffs	Cuff Flaps
1	Scarlet	Scarlet	Scarlet
2	Scarlet	Scarlet	Blue
3	Scarlet	Blue	Scarlet
4	Light orange	Light orange	Light orange
7	Yellow	Yellow	Yellow
8	Yellow	Yellow	Blue
11	Pink	Pink	Blue
12	Pink	Blue	Pink

Officers: In appearance, they resembled the enlisted men. The cuirass was often more elaborately finished and decorated, the same was true for the helmet, where a plume was attached. They also had silver-plated rank insignia. For service in the field, the pants were usually dark blue.

The cloth shabraque and pistol holster covers were also dark blue and trimmed with a wide silver border.

Trumpeter: In 1815, as in other regiments, the uniform differed by the color of the *livree*, which could also have different features or designs. The helmet usually had a white horsehair tail and occasionally a colored plume.

Carabiniers

The two regiments took part in the campaign. They were considered an elite force in the army and had an unofficial Guard status.

Uniforms and equipment

They received their distinctive white uniform after 1809, still typical were the brass helmets with a red *chenille* crest. Both regiments had light blue distinctions on the coat's collar and turn-backs. The regimental distinction was only apparent on the cuff, which for the 1st Regiment was red with white flaps and piped sky blue. In the 2nd Regiment, the cuffs were sky blue with flaps of the same color and white piping. However, the cuirasses were also brass. The trousers were gray or grayish brown, worn with high top boots.

The bandoliers were ocher with white edging. As a cutting weapon they had the straight saber and as a firearm the carbine. The shabraques with sheepskin were like those of the cuirassiers, but in light blue cloth with white trim and grenade emblems in the corners.

Officers: The helmet and coat cut were like those of the enlisted men, in addition, the pants were also in white in the field. The cuirass was more elaborately finished, e.g. with the retaining straps, and it also had a sun-shaped plate in the upper chest area. The epaulettes were silver. The light blue cloth shabraque also had a silver border.

Trumpeters: In the 1st Regiment they wore the green *livree*, but with white braids edged in red and distinction color in red. In the 2nd regiment they also wore the green *livree*, but in this case with yellow braids and emblems and distinctions in sky blue.

Dragoons

Organization

Of the 24 regiments that existed in the Empire, nine were disbanded in 1814.

Uniforms and equipment

They kept the characteristic green uniforms and the brass helmets, but they were equipped with a horse tail. Also here the plume was no longer attached.

The coat with closed lapels had short coattails. The colored distinctions were on the collar, lapels and the cuffs. The color of the cuff flaps varied according to the table shown below. The grenade emblems were green. Gray, beige or brown overalls were worn, along with the high boots.

The forming of elite companies and whether they were equipped with bearskin caps or epaulettes is not clear. The dragoons also included sappers, but it is not clear to what extent in 1815 they were equipped separately.

Armament consisted of a heavy straight dragoon saber and the dragoon musket, as they were originally intended to be mounted infantry.

Like for the cuirassiers, they had sheepskin saddlecloth covers with cloth attachments, but they were green.

Distinction Colors:

Regiment	Lapels and Turnbacks	Collar	Cuffs	Cuff Flaps
2	Scarlet	Green	Scarlet	Green
4	Scarlet	Scarlet	Scarlet	Scarlet
5	Scarlet	Green	Scarlet	Green
6	Scarlet	Scarlet	Green	Scarlet
7	Crimson	Crimson	Crimson	Crimson
11	Crimson	Green	Crimson	Green
12	Crimson	Crimson	Green	Crimson
13	Pink	Pink	Pink	Pink
14	Pink	Green	Pink	Green
15	Pink	Pink	Green	Pink
16	Pink	Pink	Green	Pink
17	Pink	Green	Pink	Green
20	Yellow	Green	Yellow	Green

Officers: They wore the same uniform as the enlisted men. The single-breasted surtout was often used as a variant for field service. The rank insignia and emblems were silver. The saber belt and gauntlets were available in white as well as black leather. The rectangular dark green cloth shabraque had a silvered border.

Trumpeters: Uniforms as for the cuirassiers. However, the coat colors and equipment differed for the regiments. In some regiments they wore red or white epaulettes to identify them. The saddlery was covered with a black sheepskin.

Light cavalry

Chevau-Légers Lanciers

Organization

It was not until 1811 that this branch, light cavalry lancers, was created by conversion from and reorganization of a number of dragoon regiments. They were intended to reinforce the light cavalry and to fight the enemy more effectively, especially with their lances. Furthermore, they supported the heavy regiments as flank protection. During the Restoration, six of the nine regiments were transferred to the Royal Army without major changes. All the regiments took part in the 1815 campaign.

Uniforms, equipment

The headgear was the dragoon model helmet made of brass, but with a black *chenille* crest. A special feature was the crest color for the elite company of the 6th Regiment, which was made of red wool.
The Spencer coat had the dark green color of the light cavalry with distinctions on the collar, lapels, cuffs and turnbacks. In the field, the lapels were often folded back, leaving the green inside exposed and the distinction color visible only as the outside edge. The elite company wore red wool epaulettes instead of shoulder straps.
The leather equipment was white.
However, there was an exception in the 6th Regiment in the color of the leather equipment and gloves, which were ocher.

Distinctions:

Regiment	Distinction color
1	Dark red
2	Bright orange
3	Pink
4	Light red
5	Light blue
6	Light red

The long dark green or gray overalls usually had a black leather reinforcement on the inside and a stripe in regimental color on the outside seam.

The main armament was the lance, which had a white and red lance pennon at the upper end, plus a light cavalry saber. A dragoon model musket or an equestrian pistol, which was hooked on the bandolier, served as a firearm. The saddle pad was made of white sheepskin with colored edging.

Officers: The helmet had a cover of imitation leopard skin and a larger *chenille* crest crest. The rank insignia and trimmings were gold colored. The cartridge pouch bandoliers, in addition to black, were often made of red colored leather with gilded trim. Tight green breeches with short Hungarian boots were usually worn. Long overalls with double piping on the outside seam were also used. The officers of the 6th Regiment distinguished themselves by wearing madder red pants. Black leather gauntlets were also fashionable, and the cloth shabraques were pointed.

Trumpeter liverees:

Regiment	Helmet Crest	Coat Color	Distinction Color	Border on collar and Lapels	Special Features
1	White	Dark blue	Red	White	White epaulettes
1 variant	White	Green	Red	Yellow with embroidery - emblem N (for Napoleon) and eagle	Coat with lapels in red, Red epaulettes
2	White	Blue		White	White epaulettes
3		Imperial	Livree	Yellow with embroidery - emblem N (for Napoleon) and eagle	Single-breasted coat
4	Black	Imperial	Livree	Yellow with embroidery - emblem N (for Napoleon) and eagle	Single-breasted coat
5	Black	Imperial	Livree	Yellow with embroidery - emblem N (for Napoleon) and eagle	Single-breasted coat
6	Red	Red	Green	Border in yellow	Red pants

Hussars

Organization

In 1814, this type of regiment was also severely reduced, so that of the 14 formations formed in the late phase of the empire, only six regiments remained. In the Waterloo campaign, five of these regiments were deployed, although only the 7th Regiment fought directly in the battle.

Uniforms and equipment

By the spring of 1815, the uniform had not changed conspicuously, except for the royal emblems. The hussars were able to retain a certain glamor of bygone years, in their original Hungarian-style dress, and still stood out with the different color schemes of the regiments. The headgear was also fashionable and corresponded to the new cylindrical model (Shako Rouleau) introduced in 1812-1813, which had a colored body.

The shako was covered with red cloth, with the 7th Regiment having a special cover in green. The 1810 model was also still in use and mostly with a cloth or oilcloth cover. The busby was still used sporadically by the elite companies. The dolman was in the regimental and associated distinction color, the pelisse also in a specific color as indicated in the following table. However, this was not usually worn in the field, except for officers.

The breeches had different variants, such as in the basic color of the dolman (sky or dark blue). The overalls with leather inserts, which were also available in red, were preferred by the officers. The armament was the same as in the light cavalry with a saber and carbine. The sabretache, which was covered with black leather, had the regimental number or the stylized eagle as a fitting.

In bad weather they wore the green overcoat, which was also worn rolled over the shoulder. The saddle cover, made of white sheepskin, had a jagged border in regimental color.

Distinction colors:

Regiment	Dolman	Collar	Cuffs	Laces & Frogging
1	Sky blue	Sky blue	Red	White
4	Dark blue	Dark blue	Red	Yellow
5	Medium blue	Medium blue	White	Yellow
6	Red	Dark blue	Dark blue	Yellow
7	Green	Red	Red	Yellow

Regiment	Pelisse	Overalls	Valise	Sheepskin Trim
1	Sky blue	Sky blue	Blue	Red
2	Red	Dark blue	Blue	Red
5	White	Medium blue	Medium blue	Light blue
6	Dark blue	Dark blue	Red	Red
7	Green	Red	Red	Green

For officers, all laces and frogging were gold or silver, analogous to the color of the regiment's braid. The rank insignia in the form of chevrons could be seen on sleeves and trouser trimmings. The shabraques were made of cloth.

The trumpeters, especially among the hussars, wore different color uniforms but these are not consistently documented for 1815:

Regiment	Shako Cover	Dolman	Pelisse	Lace & Frogging	Pants
1	Red	Medium blue	White	White / Red	Red
1 variation	Busby	Medium blue	White	Red	Red
2	Red	Red	Dark blue	Yellow	Dark blue
6	Black	Dark blue	Red	Yellow	Dark blue
6 variation	Busby	Red	Red	Yellow	Dark blue
7	Light green	Green		Yellow	Red

To what extent the imperial *livree* was used by individual companies cannot be determined with certainty. The trumpet cord made of twisted cord had variants, for example they were solid red, yellow and green or yellow and red. The shabraques with black sheepskin had a jagged red border.

Chasseurs à Cheval

Organization

Even in this light cavalry branch, only 15 regiments remained out of about thirty. Of these, eight took part in the 1815 campaign.

Uniforms and equipment

After initial diversity in the uniform patterns, the chasseurs had achieved the first extensive standardization in appearance with the regulation of 1812. Thus, the coat, closed at the front, worn with long overalls, both in dark green basic color, became the typical feature for these units.

The headgear was the shako Model 1812, which was often worn with a cover. Occasionally, the successor model, the tall cylindrical shako, was also worn. An exception was the 1st Regiment, which had received a tall *chenille* crested helmet in 1814 as a royal unit and also wore it on the campaign.

The elite company (1st company of the 1st Squadron) officially wore red bands on the shako and red epaulettes, but for these companies the busby was still common as headgear.

The green coats usually had the lapels folded over, so only the colored outer seam was visible. The distinctions varied from regiment to regiment being all in the regimental color or green piped in the distinction color.

Single-breasted jackets *(surtout)* were still widespread. All models were decorated with the colored distinctions of the respective regiment on the collar, cuffs and coattails.

Usually long green or gray overalls with leather inserts and side stripes were worn. The green overcoat was worn rolled-up over the shoulder.

Distinctions:

Regiment	Collar and Turnbacks	Cuffs	Piping on Lapels
1	Scarlet	Scarlet	Scarlet
3	Scarlet	Green with red piping	Scarlet
4	Yellow	Yellow	Yellow
6	Yellow	Yellow	Yellow
8	Green with pink piping	Pink	Pink
9	Pink	Green with pink piping	Pink
11	Green with crimson piping	Crimson	Crimson
12	Crimson	Green, with crimson piping	Crimson

The white sheepskin saddle pads had a colored serrated border in regimental distinction color.

Officers: The uniform was like that of the enlisted men but with silver-colored rank insignia. As headgear, the new shako (rouleau) was already very common, decorated with cording. The red cloth shabraques of the 1st Regiment, tapering to the rear, differed from the green cloth ones of the other regiments, which were also trimmed with a silver-colored border.

Trumpeters: In the 1st Regiment, they wore a helmet with a red *chenille* crest, a single-breasted blue coat with red distinctions, and had a white collar with red intermittent braid. The trumpet had a white cord.

Artillery

Organization

Napoleon had to reorganize this branch of the army as well, since it had been neglected under the Bourbons. Thus, trained crews were lacking, as were draft horses. Equipment was completed where possible and the scarce ammunition was replenished. For the Northern Army, 246 guns could be assembled. In some cases, batteries were reduced to six guns, resulting in a varying number of batteries per division. The artillery system of 1803 had two calibers - the 12-pounder and the 6-pounder guns.

In June 1815, eight regiments of foot artillery and four of horse artillery were available for the campaign.

Uniforms and equipment

In terms of clothing, this branch followed the pattern of the line infantry, and the horse artillerymen followed the example of the chasseurs à cheval. The traditional color, even before the Revolution, was the dark blue coat with pants of the same color. The collar and the turnbacks had the basic red color of the technical troops. However, the lapels - in the coat's basic color - were piped red.

The dark blue pants were tight-fitting, though in the field the loose-fitting pantaloons, usually with red side stripes, were common.

The equipment was like that of the infantry. The sword knots was always red. However, the overcoat had a dark blue basic color.

Mounted units' uniforms followed the pattern of the light cavalry with pointed cuffs, long overalls, and sabers.

Officers in the mounted batteries often used the busby with red bag as headgear. Many company officers used the *surtout* for service in the field, which was dark blue. Long blue or gray pants with wide gold side stripes were introduced for officers in foot units.

Artillery Train

Organization

Savings were made in the technical units in 1814 and the train was reduced to eight battalions of four companies each. For the 1815 campaign, each company was assigned individually to the batteries and acted with its own officers, depending on the needs of the artillery.

Uniforms and equipment

The uniform and equipment were like the horse artillery. The coat pattern had lapels or was single-breasted. The coat's basic color was iron-gray with dark blue distinctions, which were partially trimmed with white piping. Trousers were pants with or without leather trim and worn with high boots. The armament was usually the short saber on the waist belt. Officers had silver-colored rank insignia and armament similar to that of the mounted chasseurs.

Génie/Engineers

Organization

Napoleon retained the organization with three regiments that had been introduced in 1814. He distributed the 18 companies among the five corps and attached them to the artillery. Their real task was to clear obstacles or build simple fortifications. Some of them were equipped with axes, picks and shovels which the men carried themselves. A separate train for this purpose did not exist. The reason for attaching them to the artillery was more to increase the latter's firepower, since there were no tasks for this special branch in the campaign.

Uniforms and equipment

It was identical to that of the artillery on foot, except for the distinctions, which here was black piped with red.

Column Train

Organization

In October 1814 there were still 26 companies, which in 1815 were assigned to the individual corps, company by company, usually with 40 wagons.
These units were responsible for transporting food, equipment and luggage. The train was divided into five sections for the transportation of certain types of supplies, such as meat, bread, wine, feed for animals and material for uniforms and other equipment.

Uniforms

Like the artillery train but the coat had reddish brown distinctions.

Medical Service

Medical personnel in the French Army were better trained and more efficient in treating the wounded than those in their Allied opponents. The medical corps consisted branches of surgeons, physicians and lastly pharmacists. Each division in turn had three classes divided by function, rank, and skill (1st–3rd class). Outstanding for his time was the Chief Surgeon, Baron Larrey, who did much for an organized structure and methods of treatment.

In addition, there were the detachments of stretcher bearers who were to carry the wounded to the field hospitals or wagons. These companies had been formed in 1813 to support the medical officers and were attached to the army corps or divisions. Independently of this, each regiment had its own medical staff.

Uniforms

Starting in 1803, all officers wore the medium blue single-breasted coat, with or without lace on the buttonholes. The distinctions on the collar and cuffs for medical officers were black, for surgeons red and for pharmacists green. On the distinctions were yellow double strands, which, depending on the number, designated the different ranks. As headgear they used the bicorne hat and as trousers gray or blue overalls in the field.

The stretcher bearers were dressed like the infantry but with brown coats and red distinctions. As equipment they were each equipped with a "half" stretcher, which consisted of a bar and a cloth sling. However, only a small number of wounded could be recovered in this manner. The extent to which these stretcher bearers were in action in 1815 is not documented.

The text below the illustrations on the following pages was not by Charles Lyall.
Those texts were written by the authors.

UNIFORMS OF THE ARMIES AT WATERLOO

VOLUME 4
THE FRENCH ARMY

AS DRAWN BY
CHARLES LYALL
1894

Napoleon I, Emperor of France

Napoleon Bonaparte, unlike his adversary Wellington, preferred to lead from a position in the rear and was therefore south of La Belle Alliance near the Decoster house from about 2:00 p.m. on June 18, 1815. From the elevation there, he had a good view of Hougoumont and La Haye Sainte, as well as the area between these two reference points on the battlefield

Uniform: In the field, Napoleon wore the undress uniform of the Chasseurs à Cheval of the Guard under his gray greatcoat and the distinctive simple bicorne hat. Lyall did, however, use some imagination here in this portrait at least with the coat, because the dark green coat had tapered, dark green lapels with red piping. The collar was also red. The buttons were gilded, as shown here.
The French cockade is missing on the bicorne hat and the greatcoat buttons were usually covered with the same cloth of the coat. The blue shabraque cloth should actually be crimson.

Maréchal de l'Empire in Undress Uniform When Mounted

In the 1815 campaign, Napoleon was accompanied by three marshals (*maréchal de l'empire*) with the Northern Army. First of all, Jeande-Dieu Soult, who replaced Berthier, the long-time chief of the general staff. Then the tragic figure of Maréchal Michel Ney, who during the memorable confrontation with Napoleon changed sides during the march to Paris and had to atone for this with his death. Finally, there is Emmanuel de Grouchy, freshly promoted to Maréchal in 1815, who was accused by Napoleon on St. Helena of being partly responsible for the defeat at Waterloo..

Uniform: Lyall shows a marshal in his undress uniform, which could have been worn at Waterloo, but is more likely the "frac" (frock coat) described in the text. The coat's rich, golden embroidery is recognizable here but the cuffs are not correctly depicted, these should be straight and provided with golden piping and two rows of decorative braids.

Aide de Camp of a Maréchal de Camp

In the French Empire, the number of aides de camp was linked to the rank of their superior officer. Thus, a *Maréchal de l'Empire* was supposed to have six, a *Général de Division* three and a *Maréchal de Camp* (formerly *Général de Brigade*) two aides de camp. However, the marshals in particular clearly exceeded this prescribed number.

Uniform: Lyall probably used a plate from the work of Vernet-Lami as a model, which shows an Aide de Camp of a Général de Brigade in 1812. However, Lyall changed the pointed end of the lapels shown there into the variant shown here, which is not documented. Lyall did not adopt the prescribed sky-blue armband and a cartridge pouch bandolier covered with red leather from the original plate. The pants shown here could also have been worn in this style by the Aides de Camp in 1815, deviating from the style described in the text.

Grenadier of the Imperial Guard in a Greatcoat

The two battalions of the 1st Regiment remained in their reserve positions throughout the Battle of Waterloo, forming squares near Decoster's house in the evening. The two battalions of the 2nd Guards Grenadier Regiment of the Old Guard were deployed earlier. The 1st Battalion, together with the 1st Battalion of the 1st Chasseurs of the Guard, was able to make a successful counterattack in Plancenoit. The 2nd Battalion was deployed to cover the general retreat.

Uniform: Lyall wanted to depict a grenadier of the line infantry, judging from his caption. However, it is inserted here since the line grenadiers no longer wore bearskin caps and the appearance more closely resembled that of the grenadiers of the Guard. This uniform in the regulation double-breasted, but dark blue, greatcoat corresponds to an image of the Guard Grenadiers of 1815. The dark blue pants were more common in the 1st Regiment. However, the cap had an emblem with an eagle and grenades.

Grenadier of the Imperial Guard in the Dress Uniform

The two regiments of the Middle Guard were employed in the final assault against the Anglo-Allied Line deployed and their retreat initiated the general disintegration of the French line. The single battalion of the 4th and the 1st Battalion of the 3rd Regiments were part of the assault column; the 2nd Battalion of the 3rd Guards was to stabilize the wavering front between Hougoumont and La Haye Sainte but was almost completely wiped out in the square formation.

Uniform: Lyall shows here a Guard Grenadier in his dress uniform, which was certainly not worn in this form at Waterloo. Only the coat, actually with red cuffs and white cuff flaps and red turnbacks could be part of the uniform worn at that time. The orange chevrons on the left arm distinguish 15-20 years length of service. The bearskin cap was worn without the cording and plume in 1815.

Grenadier of the Imperial Guard in the Dress Uniform

Uniform: Lyall assigns this grenadier to the Old Guard, either the 1st or 2nd Guard Grenadier Foot (à pied) Regiment. In contrast to the previous Guard Grenadier, the coat is correctly depicted here with red cuffs and white cuff flaps. Only, the coattails' white piping seems to be on the outside here, which is wrong from the pattern, as it ran along the inside of the coattails. However, the grenadiers did not go into the campaign with the cording on the bearskin cap, also the white pants and especially white gaiters of the parade uniform would not have been worn. On the musket shown here, the fittings are incorrectly colored, as they had to be made of brass.

Tirailleur of the Imperial Guard around 1813

All units of the Young Guard Division, consisting of Tirailleurs and Voltigeurs, were the first of the Guard units to be deployed at Waterloo, namely at Plancenoit at about 6:00 p.m. They fought there against the advancing Prussian troops for the remainder of the battle until the general retreat of the French.

Uniform: The shako shown with (an actually inverted) "V" wasreplaced in 1813 by a plain black shako with no cording and a red pompom. Lyall still has the coat in the old pattern (until 1813–1814), but the lapels would have to be pointed towards the bottom. The coat lacks the blue piping on the collar and the white piping on the pointed cuffs. The black gaiters would have to be cut to a 'V' at the top at the front.

Chasseurs à Pied of the Imperial Guard

The chasseur regiments of the Old Guard were initially held back as reserves. While the 1st Battalion of the 1st Regiment did not fight the advancing Prussians until late in the evening or at night, the 2nd Battalion moved up to support the attack of the Middle Guard and got caught in the middle of the French infantrymen flooding back in disarray. The 1st Battalion of the 2nd Regiment was employed in the fighting at Plancenoit, the 2nd Battalion met the same fate as their 1st Regiment counterparts.

Uniform: The chasseur presented by Lyall is quite consistent for the 1815 campaign, with a few minor errors. The white cording on the cap was no longer worn, feather plumes were available but it is unclear whether they were worn. The epaulette's crescent should be red. The short saber did not have three ribs on the basket. The breeches and gaiters are correct but the majority of chasseurs à pied went to the field in blue pants.

Chasseurs à Pied of the Imperial Guard

Uniform: In the original caption, this chasseur is described as a member of the Old Guard, i.e. from the 1st or 2nd Chasseurs à Pied Regiment. This chasseur's coat, in contrast to the previous figure, is properly colored with red cuffs and turnbacks, as well as the white pointed lapels with red piping. But here, too, the crescent of the epaulette should be red, only the slider was green for the Guard chasseurs à pied. The cap's plume is correctly depicted and it may have been worn at Waterloo, but the white cording certainly was not. The musket fittings should be brass.

Chasseurs à Pied of the Imperial Guard, Sapper

All four battalions of the 3rd and 4th Regiments participated in the Middle Guard's attack on the British lines, where they suffered substantial losses. By June 26, only about one-fifth of the original strength remained under arms. In particular, the two units of the 4th Regiment, consolidated into one large battalion, suffered significant casualties from the flanking fire of the 52nd Line Regiment.

Uniform: Even though the regulations required two sappers per company, only the two regiments of Chasseurs à Pied of the Guard went into the campaign of 1815 with the Old Guard. Lyall has allowed some mistakes. For example, the bearskin cap had no cap plate and the cording may not have been worn. The rather lighter brown apron was worn under the coat. The sappers' coat itself was trimmed with gold braid on collars, lapels and turnbacks. Gold colored crossed axes were attached t the upper sleeves. The epaulettes were gold and had red and gold fringes and green sliders.

Voltigeur of the Imperial Guard, 1st Voltigeur Regiment

Together with the comrades of the tirailleurs, the two voltigeur regiments also went into battle against the Prussians at Plancenoit around 6:00 p.m. They fought the entire further course there until the general retreat of the French.

Uniform: At least in its basic appearance, Lyall's uniform matches that worn by the soldiers of the 1st Regiment in 1815. The shako is correctly depicted except for the cording. With the coat, however, the pattern is incorrect, since the voltigeurs and the tirailleurs went into the campaign with so-called "Bardin" coats. Those coats had dark blue lapels that reached all the way down, so the vest shown here was no longer visible. The pointed red cuffs should actually be piped white. The collar, however, is wrong, as it was yellow with blue piping. Instead of the tight pants, the voltigeurs wore long white pants over the gaiters. The short saber is wrong, as hilt of the "Sabre briquet" had a knuckle guard without branches.

Voltigeurs of the Imperial Guard, Voltigeur in the Dress Uniform

Uniform: The guardsman is completely correct for the period until 1813. For 1815, in addition to the closed coat, the shako was worn without cording and plume. The epaulettes would have to been all in green. The saber tassel is missing and should be made of green wool. As additional equipment, the voltigeurs also carried water bottles of various models as well as cooking utensils, attached to the knapsack.
(Source: Martinet's series of plates)

Voltigeurs of the Imperial Guard, Company-Grade Officer

Uniform: Depicted correctly as a whole for the dress uniform until 1812. In 1815, officers in the Young Guard also wore the Bardin pattern coat with long coattails. However, six buttons would have been visible on each lapel. In the field, the shako without decoration or the bicorne hat was used as headgear. On duty and in the field, the gorget was worn as additional rank insignia. Voltigeur officers' armament was the saber with gold-plated tassel.

Marine of the Imperial Guard in the Dress Uniform

Even though the marines were subordinate to the Engineers (*Génie*) of the Imperial Guard, they were considered more of an infantry unit and were used as such at Waterloo. After being in reserve for almost the entire course of the battle, they took on missions in the rearguard to cover the general French retreat.

Uniform: Lyall shows a marine in a dress uniform with almost no flaws. However, the marines at Waterloo probably did not deploy in this attractive uniform but went on the campaign with overcoats or a simple dark blue Spencer. The errors in the representation of the dress uniform are the wrong coloring of the bands on the shako, which should be orange, and the decoration on the thighs, which should display Hungarian knots.

Chasseurs à Cheval of the Imperial Guard, Officer

The Chasseurs à Cheval Regiment was commanded by the Commander of the Light Cavalry Division of the Imperial Guard, *Général de Division* Lefebvre-Desnouettes during the second wave of the major cavalry attack on the Anglo-Allied lines between Hougoumont and La Haye Sainte.

Uniform: Lyall was guided here, as in some other depictions, by models of guardsmen from the time before 1815. The officers in the campaign of 1815 are also likely to have worn green overalls with leather reinforcements. It is also unclear whether they wore the pelisse. The officers' sabretache was also made of black leather and had a yellow metal eagle on it. The dolman's collar would have to be green with gold edging. Finally, in 1815, the officers' busby was worn with no plume and probably no busby bag. The brass eagle on the busby shown here by Lyall is also incorrect even for the earlier era. In addition, the saber had only a simple knuckle guard without branches.

Chevau-Légers Lanciers Polonais of the Imperial Guard, Lancer

The squadron of Polish Lancers, only 115 strong, was deployed with the Red Lancers' other four squadrons in the major cavalry charge against the Anglo-Allied lines.

Uniform: The soldier shown here is depicted by Lyall in dress uniform. Whether they went into battle in this uniform is not very likely. For example, the czapka would have been worn without cording and plume but with a black oilcloth cover. Instead of the leather chinstrap, the czapka had silver chin-scales. The kurtka may have been worn folded back, so that only a narrow crimson edging was visible on the outside. The actual blue trousers of the dress uniform were replaced in the field by blue overalls with leather reinforcing and crimson outside stripes decorated with pewter buttons.

Chevau-Légers Lanciers Polonais of the Imperial Guard, Officer

The staff officers of the Polish squadron in 1815 were *Chef d'escadron* (squadron commander) Jerzmanowski and Major Raoul. A striking figure was given by Captain Szulc, who was 2.13 meters (7-foot) tall.

Uniform: Here, too, Lyall was tempted to depict the dress uniform with some errors. The officers also probably fought in 1815 in a less elaborate outfit. The czapka was worn without the cording and plume; perhaps the officers dispensed with the cover and displayed the crimson top with silver braid trim. The black body with gilded sun emblem was separated from upper shell by a silver stripe. The kurtka collar was trimmed with silver braid like the lapels. The retaining cords would have to be silver, on the left was a silver epaulet according to rank. The sash is not documented. In the field, officers wore blue pants with two crimson stripes on the sides.

Chevau-Légers Lanciers Rouges of the Imperial Guard, Lancer

The Red Lancer (*Chevau-Légers Lanciers Rouges*) or "Dutch" Regiment attacked the right center of the Anglo-Allied lines during the major French cavalry charge and also ran into a square of Brunswick infantry.

Uniform: Lyall shows here a soldier in a uniform that would be wrong even for a parade uniform. On the one hand, the gold-red waistbelt, which is worn by officers in a narrower form, is conspicuous in that the enlisted men had a white waistbelt. The Red Lancers' czapka had a scarlet top, the cording and plume would also have to be white, however these were not worn, instead the czapka was probably protected by a black wax cover. The kurtka's medium blue distinctions should be dark blue, the epaulet on the right should be yellow with a dark blue crescent. The yellow retaining cords are missing on the left. In the 1815 campaign, overalls were indeed worn, but they were dark blue with black leather reinforcement and scarlet outer stripes with brass buttons.

Chevau-Légers Lanciers Rouges of the Imperial Guard, Officer

Uniform: A staff officer is shown here, as can be seen from the epaulettes with thick fringes, but these should only be worn on the left side. Officers had a gold retaining cord on the right shoulder. The czapka should have a cover made of scarlet cloth and only the corners and edges were covered with gold braid. Also the officers should have folded the dark blue lapels in the field to have only one dark blue edge visible under the scarlet outer cloth. The parade uniform pants shown here would have been replaced in the field by dark blue trousers with gold braid trim on the outer seams. The bandolier and narrower waistbelt is gilded with narrow red stripes is confirmed by a depiction by É. Detaille. In the field, however, officers would have replaced them with ones of whitened leather or at least protected the cartridge pouch bandolier with a red leather cover.

Chevau-Légers Lanciers Rouges of the Imperial Guard, Trumpeter

Uniform: As with the chasseurs à cheval, there are no indications for 1815 as to what the trumpeters of the Polish and Red Lancers looked like. However, it is likely that the trumpeter shown here went on campaign in the undress uniform with a light blue kurtka. Like here, the white kurtka had scarlet lapels, collar, piping and pointed cuffs. However, these would have to be trimmed with gold braid around the edges. Like the enlisted men and officers, the trumpeters would probably have worn the lapels folded over, so that an almost the entire light blue kurtka was visible. The overalls shown correctly here would have to be dark blue with a red outer stripe. The waistbelt would be narrower and made of white leather with gilded belt buckle. Probably a red epaulette with yellow fringes was worn on the right and red and yellow retaining cords on the left shoulder.

Empress' Dragoon Regiment, Dragoon

The Dragoons of the Imperial Guard, along with the Horse Grenadiers, were thrown into the ongoing cavalry fighting against the Anglo-Allied forces late in the afternoon.

Uniform: Lyall shows, almost correctly, the uniform with which the Guard Dragoons went on campaign. However, the coat did not have a red collar, this was green and instead the turnbacks would have been red. The helmet corresponds to the appearance to that of the dragoon but it remains unclear whether the red plume was actually worn on the campaign. The belt buckle showed an imprinted grenade; and the dragoon straight saber had a grenade ornament affixed in the basket. The pants would have been made of gray cloth.

Empress' Dragoon Regiment, Staff Officer

Uniform: The officers, like the enlisted men, probably went to the campaign with their coats, though the single-breasted dark green surtout would have also been possible, but both with green collars. Both coats had gilded buttons and, depending on the rank, gilded epaulettes on the left shoulder and gilded retaining cords on the right shoulder. The officers are also likely to have gone on campaign wearing gray breeches, alternatively the light beige breeches as shown here by Lyall would have been possible. The red plume is likely to have been removed as in the other cavalry units. The gilded belt buckle would have shown a grenade.

Empress' Dragoon Regiment, Trumpeter

Uniform: Like most NCOs, the trumpeters also wore a single-breasted surtout. In contrast to the parade coat shown here, this was sky blue and had a crimson collar and cuffs that were edged in gold. The turnbacks, also crimson, had gold grenades as emblems. The epaulettes and retaining cord were mixed crimson and gold. The helmet, as shown here, had a white horsehair tail, and the plume was probably not worn. The trumpeters also wore gray cloth pants, instead of the white ones shown here. The belt buckle is also shown incorrectly here – it had an engraved grenade.

Grenadier à Cheval of the Imperial Guard

Late in the afternoon, the Guards Horse Grenadiers were committed along with the Dragoons and the *Gendarmerie d'Élite* in support of the French cavalry charges against the Anglo-Allied lines and became disorganized.

Uniform: Lyall's depiction is close to the actual appearance of the Guard Horse Grenadiers. The black bearskin cap had neither cording nor plume. However, the cap cover had an orange cross instead of the grenade shown here. The coat is shown correctly but the epaulettes were orange, and the retaining cord on the right shoulder would be of the same color. The cartridge pouch did not have an eagle, but a diamond-shaped plate with three stars and coat-of-arms badge. The straight saber was worn on the waistbelt and not on a bandolier. The gray trousers are correctly depicted.

Gendarme d'Élite of the Imperial Guard

Although the duties of the Elite Gendarmerie were more akin to traditional police activities, they were attached to the Horse Grenadiers at Waterloo and participated in the major cavalry charges against the Anglo-Allied line.

Uniform: The gendarme shown here roughly corresponds to the appearance as they rode to the 1815 campaign. The coat is correctly depicted except for the actual white metal buttons, also the white retaining cords belong on the left shoulder. Instead of this coat, a single-breasted surtout could also have been worn. The cartridge pouch bandolier, however, would have been buff with white borders. The headgear, the bearskin cap of the former gendarmes until 1814, is shown here. These should have been present in 1815, but probably these were no longer issued and the gendarmes rode to Belgium with a metal helmet of the Bourbon gendarmerie. The straight saber's basket should show a grenade.

Foot Artillery of the Guard, Gunner

Three batteries of the Imperial Guard were ordered by Napoleon to join the "Great Battery", which formed up between 1:00 and 1:30 p.m. opposite the Anglo-Allied line. There the 6th Company formed the left wing of the artillery line.

Uniform: The uniform of the Guard Foot Artillery is well represented here by Lyall. The cap conforms to regulation, probably the bearskin hat had only a black top with no emblem. The coat would have to have straight red cuffs with red flaps though. The dark blue vest was visible under the lapels which were not cut so high, but it had no red piping. The pants were looser and worn over the gaiters.

Foot Artillery of the Guard, Officer

Uniform: Lyall does a good job with this uniform, since the bearskin hat's cording was gold, although it and the plume may have been removed due to the rainy weather. The coat would have to have straight red cuffs like for the gunner, and there were red cuff flaps with three buttons. Lyall also has forgotten the three large buttons, gilded for officers, below the seam of the right lapel. Unlike enlisted men, officers tucked their pants into their boots, but these had light brown cuffs. The officer shown here is likely to be a staff officer based on the thick bouillon fringes.

Horse Artillery of the Guard, Gunner

The four batteries of Guard Horse Artillery were held in reserve and also did not accompany the French cavalry's attacks. It is not clear whether they were present in the evening at the attack of the Middle Guard.

Uniform: The cannoneer shown here does not correspond in appearance to that of 1815. Lyall has been guided here by representations, such as the series of Vernet-Lami, which he used more frequently. There an artilleryman of the Guard Horse Artillery is also seen from the left side, but mounted. Lyall has largely correctly used that gunner in his standing figure, but this uniform was only worn until 1814. In the 1815 campaign, the gunners had neither dolman nor pelisse, but a dark blue coat. Also the tight pants were replaced by overalls with leather reinforcements.

Engineers *(Génie)* of the Imperial Guard, Sapper

The Guard Sappers had no role as engineers at Waterloo; they were only involved, together with the marines, at Ligny in an attack by the Guards. At Waterloo they covered the retreat of the French troops from the battlefield in the late evening.

Uniform: Lyall's depiction captures well the appearance of the sappers, who for 1815 were described in a plate by Genty. The metal helmet with brass crest, brass eagle as an emblem, black chenille crest and red plume is correctly depicted here. The coat with the black distinctions should have red piping on the collar, the lapels and cuffs. The lapels are cut a little too high here and the blue vest was visible with three buttons. The blue pants were also tucked into black gaiters.

Line Infantry, Colonel

The main burden in battles was borne by the line infantry, including the fighting at Waterloo. The assaults on Hougoumont and La Haye Sainte were carried out under difficult conditions and with heavy losses. The d'Erlon Corps' advance in the afternoon was also carried out with great bravado but failed due to the actions of the Allied cavalry. The colonel was the commander of the regiment, represented by the major, who was also the second highest staff officer.

Uniform: As in the following depictions, the lapels would have been closed. The number of buttons is incomplete, six on each side would be correct. The cuffs were always white and trimmed with red. The shako's plume should be white and for a major a red tip would be correct. In the field, the single-breasted coat (surtout) was also worn and the shako plume removed.
(Source: according to Édouard Detaille)

Line Infantry, Sapper

Each regiment had four sappers per battalion, who were responsible for removing entanglements and obstacles or for the construction of barricades and light fortifications. The sapper typically appeared with fur cap, full beard, apron and axe. Thus, they were used alongside the engineers/*Génie* in the battle for the two farms complexes.

Uniform: In the line units, besides the tall fur cap, the shako could be seen in 1815. The busby was more in use in the light infantry. Considering the supply situation, however, the busby is quite conceivable. Instead of the saber, the sapper's equipment included a fascine knife. The carbine is correct, but without the bayonet. The epaulettes should be red instead of purple.

Line infantry, Eagle-Bearer 1st Class *(premier porte-aigle)*

In April 1815, it was stipulated that one eagle bearer *(premier porte-aigle)* was to be provided for each regiment in the manning. He carried the flag, Model 1815, flanked and protected by two non-commissioned officers (*Deuxième-* and *Troisième porte-aigle*), usually with the rank of sergeants *(sergents).* They were supposed to be experienced men with long service. The eagle flag bearer held a lieutenant's rank.

Uniform: For this man, the open lapels and the number of buttons also still stand out. The piping on the cuff flaps was actually white. Since 1812, the shako cording as well as the plume were officially abolished, so for the officers the headgear would have to have a pompom in the company color. The bandolier is shown here in white, but could have been red. The flagpole would have been painted medium blue.

Line Infantry, Eagle-Bearer 2nd Class *(deuxième porte-aigle)*

The two non-commissioned officers protecting the flag were reinforced by six other soldiers, mostly corporals. Their task was to repel enemy attempts to capture the flag. Despite this additional protection, the eagles (flags) of the 45th and 105th Regiments of the d'Erlon Corps were captured during the attack and in the melee following the counterattack by the British cavalry.

Uniform: As before, the lapels would have been closed and six buttons shown on each. The shako may have been in use rather than the bearskin cap shown here. It is nice to see is the pistol holster, but the pistols are missing.

Light Infantry, Voltigeur

Although the light infantry was originally intended to be used as skirmishers in open formation, it was generally used like the line. For example, the 1st and 2nd Light Regiments of the 6th Infantry Division stormed the Hougoumont farm and fought on the outskirts with temporary success, as in the brief storming of the north gate. The light infantry units also advanced to the Allied front during the massive attack by the d'Erlon Corps.

Uniform: In addition to the closed lapels, the cuffs should be pointed, and they would also have been the same color as the coat, with white piping. In 1815, the shako was without trim and cording and the shield-shaped plate was iron colored. In addition, there was no badge on the cartridge box.

2nd Hussar Regiment, Hussar

This regiment did not participate in the 1815 campaign. Of the five regiments (1st, 4th, 5th, 6th, and 7th), all but the 7th were in the army group under Marshal Grouchy, who was pursuing the withdrawing Prussians on the right wing. The individual regiments fought on June 18 at the Battles of Wavre and Limal, where there were fierce battles at the bridge crossings of the Dyle.

Uniform: The hussar wears the classic shako model, which was prescribed by the 1812 Bardin Regulations. The colored body was common only for trumpeters. The sabretache is missing from the waist belt.

7th Hussar Regiment, Hussar

Only this regiment took part directly in the Battle of Waterloo, under the command of Colonel Marbot, with three squadrons of 439 men. It carried out reconnaissance forays to the east on the right wing and encountered the vanguard of the advancing Prussian army, which led to the initial fighting.

Uniform: The drawing gives a good representation of the appearance of the hussars of 1813-1815, such as the tall shako (rouleau), which, however, had a green body. The pelisse was probably not worn. The sabretache was made of black leather and marked with the regimental number.

Chasseurs à Cheval, Elite Company

At Waterloo, the 3rd Regiment, which was located on the right wing, had its first skirmishes with the advancing Prussian vanguard in the afternoon and soon went on the defensive. The other chasseur units (9th, 11th, and 12th Regiments) were called in as reinforcements to delay the advance beyond Plancenoit.

Uniform: Here a chasseur is shown in the field uniform. It is nice to see is the rolled overcoat as protection from saber blows, and the bandeliers with cartridge pouch and the hooked carbine are easily visible. Also the trouser trim and the side stripes in the distinction color are correctly depicted.

4th Chasseurs à Cheval Regiment, Elite Company

The chasseurs à cheval, like the hussars, were used as light cavalry for reconnaissance or as skirmishers against the enemy units. They were also used to support the Heavy Cavalry as an assault force, such as at Quatre-Bras on June 16. In the heyday of the Empire, there were over 30 of these regiments.

Uniform: The view corresponds to the prescribed uniform starting in 1812, although depicted with some peculiarities. For example, the shako should not have a white trim edge at the top. The collar had no patch or braid. The epaulettes of the elite companies were of red wool and not white as depicted. The eagle-shaped shako plate was used only by the Guard.

4th Chasseurs à Cheval Regiment, Trumpeter

The 4th Regiment was one of the seven regiments that took part in the campaign. With the 9th Regiment, it formed a brigade of the 3rd Cavalry Division and was present at the 16 June Battle of Ligny.

Uniform: The same points apply as for the previous plate (4th Chasseurs à Cheval Regiment, Elite Company). The imperial livree is shown here in the simple form with braids, but without the imperial emblems. The trumpet cord would have been a mix of yellow and green.

16th Chasseurs à Cheval Regiment, Elite Company

The regiment pictured was disbanded in 1815, but some units and their elite companies still existed, which then formed the 1st Company of the 1st Squadron. The 1st and 6th Regiments (2nd Cavalry Division Piré) encountered the Dutch-Belgian cavalry at Quatre-Bras and, as the battle progressed, brought the Hanoverian battalions to heel.

Uniform: Even though the busby had already been officially abolished since 1813, it was still tolerated by regimental commanders in 1815. The folded back lapels should have a braid in the distinction color along the edge

23rd Chasseurs à Cheval Regiment, Elite Company

The regiment pictured here had also already been disbanded in 1814 under Bourbon rule. However, it could also represent the 14th Regiment, whose regimental color was light orange.

Uniform: The bandolier in the light red leather would more likely have been for an officer, however the rolled greatcoat and carbine suggest a member of the elite company. Well represented are the tight pants with the white Hungarian knots and braid, as well as the short boots with trim. The busby is unlikely to have a white plume, which was reserved for staff officers.

1st *Chevau-Légers Lanciers* Regiment, NCO

The six light horse lancer regiments were distributed among various divisions and served as reconnaissance and as support to the heavy cavalry. For example, on 16 June at Quatre-Bras, they advanced to the British line and harassed the squares or scattered the artillery crews. At Waterloo, the 3rd and 4th Regiments counterattacked the British Household Brigade and drove it back with heavy losses..

Uniform: The maréchal des logis (cavalry sergeant) rank is well recognizable by the two chevrons on the lower sleeves. The lapels would have been cut wider at the bottom. The lance flag is shown correctly, in the field this was mostly used rolled up and tied.

5th *Chevau-Légers Lanciers* Regiment, Elite Company

This regiment supported the cuirassiers' charges of the on June 16 at Quatre-Bras against the Allied line. It also attacked the squares of 42nd Highland Regiment, the Black Watch, and the 44th Foot Regiment, which held their formations with difficulty. On 18 June the 5th and 6th Companies were in a brigade of the Piré Division on the extreme left wing, at Hougoumont.

Uniform: The panel shows very well the field uniform with the plume removed, the folded over lapels and the long overalls with a wide side stripe

Dragoon of a Line Regiment in a Greatcoat

The twelve regiments in the 1815 campaign were mostly attached to the 2nd Cavalry Corps, but also assigned as reserve cavalry to the Army Department under Marshal Grouchy. For example, on June 18, the 5th, 6th, 13th, 14th, and 15th Dragoons were employed in the fighting around Wavre and further south at the bridges over the Dyle.

Uniform: This drawing does well in showing the uniform in bad weather. However, the basic color of the greatcoat with the caped shoulders would have to have been medium gray. The orange laces on the front side were exclusively for the Guard, the line units had only one row of buttons. The skull of the helmet was made of brass for the dragoons and had no imitation leopard fur trim. The plume was no longer attached in 1815.

Dragoons of the Elite Company of a Line Regiment

At the beginning of the campaign, the dragoons were deployed alongside the cuirassiers as shock cavalry. This was also the case at the Battle of Ligny on June 16 in the evening when the 5th and 6th Regiments pursued and scattered the retreating Prussian soldiers. On June 20, during Marshal Grouchy's retreat to the French border, they and the 20th Regiment were successfully engaged at Namur.

Uniform: Correctly seen are the closed lapels, however, the coattails would have been shorter. Whether fur caps were still worn by the elite in 1815 is not confirmed.

2nd Dragoon Regiment, Officer

In the Battle of Waterloo only two dragoon regiments, the 2nd and 7th, were directly involved on June 18. They were combined as a brigade in the cavalry corps under General Kellermann. In the afternoon they attacked the British squares along with the cuirassiers, but without significant success.

Uniform: This could be a lieutenant or captain in a single-breasted undress coat (surtout), which usually had no colored distinctions. He wears the straight saber, still the old model, on the belt over his shoulder. This way of wearing it was used in dismounted service. There should not be a plume on the helmet.

25th Dragoon Regiment, Officer

This regiment did not take part in the campaign.

Uniform: Overall a good depiction, but some points stand out: The waistbelt was not used, the epaulettes were of red wool for the elite, and no plume was attached.

7th Cuirassier Regiment, Staff Officer

Along with the regimental commanders, the brigade and some division generals also wore the uniform of their branch of arms or of their parent regiments. At the beginning of 1815, the cuirassiers had also been assembled from various units during mobilization and had been augmented with new recruits in order to strengthen at least the squadrons to make them operational; for example, the 7th, 11th and 12th Regiments had only two squadrons instead of the three or four they were supposed to have.

Uniform: The officer, depicted according to the source or the painting by Édouard Detaille, is absolutely correctly reproduced. The uniform shown here was still in use among commanding officers in 1815.

7th Cuirassier Regiment, Cuirassier

This regiment, after the D'Erlon Corps' failed attack in the early afternoon of 18 June, together with the 12th Cuirassiers, launched a counterattack. They encountered the British Union Brigade (dragoons and the Life Guards) and inflicted heavy casualties. During the clash they were joined by the 5th and 10th Cuirassiers and drove the British cavalry back to its original position.

Uniform: Overall, it is a correct representation, but there should be no braid on the collar and no plume on the helmet, moreover, the emblems on the turnbacks were dark blue. The trousers in chamois color were worn only with the dress uniform; in the field the gray-brown overalls were common.

7th Cuirassier Regiment, Trumpeter

During the Empire, the cuirassiers' signalmen were conspicuously distinguishable from the enlisted men by their colored coats, *chenille* crested helmets or fur caps. Many commanders invested large sums for the elaborate outfits, such as the coats with reversed distinction colors and with or without laces.

Uniform: This outfit is correct for the period 1804-1812, as a variation the yellow coat with blue trim was also worn, but the epaulettes should be fringed. Furthermore the horse tail would be white.
Source: after a series of plates by A. Martinet.

8th Cuirassier Regiment, Trumpeter

On June 16, 1815, the 8th Regiment took part in the Battle of Quatre-Bras. Under the command of General Kellermann, along with the 11th Cuirassier and other light cavalry regiments, it rode in an attack on the Allied line. Marshal Ney had given orders to break through the enemy front with just under 800 men to clear the way to Brussels. Although executed with great bravery, the attack's success was short-lived. However, the regiment captured a flag of the 69th British Infantry Regiment.

Uniform: This illustration shows nicely the coat's reversed colors with the blue laces on the chest and the piping. The white epaulettes were a distinctive insignia of the trumpeters, also here the horse tail should be in white. The white pants were worn only on gala occasions. As before, the plume should be removed. Source: from the series of plates by A. Martinet.

9th Cuirassier Regiment, Trumpeter

The 9th Regiment was not involved in the campaign in Belgium; probably this is the 1st Cuirassiers instead. This 1st Regiment, with the other eleven cavalry regiments in three divisions, made the major attacks on the Allied positions in the afternoon. They were reinforced by the carabiniers and dragoons. The attacks, carried out in three waves and with great vigor, did not achieve a successful breakthrough, but livree devolved into individual skirmishes and actions. With over 8,000 men, it was one of the last great cavalry charges of the era

Uniform: The medium blue coat with white braids may also be the simplified form of the royal livree. Also due to lack of time, only the coat's braids were changed to "neutral" white. The white epaulettes were worn by the entire regiment as a distinction and recognition awarded as the former Regiment du Roi. The helmet's tail would also have been white here. Source: according to the series of plates by A. Martinet.

12th Cuirassier Regiment, Cuirassier

Also at Ligny, on June 16, 1815, various cuirassier regiments saw action towards evening, for example, in the general attack on the retreating Prussian troops. In addition to the 12th Cuirassiers, the 9th Cuirassiers thus also overran an uhlan regiment led by Blücher, trapping the Field Marshal under his fallen horse. In the general confusion, however, this incident was not noticed by the French. Also at Waterloo, the 9th Regiment took part in the defensive attacks on the British cavalry, and later in the major attacks on the Allied lines.

Uniform: The cuirassier in field uniform is reproduced correctly as far as it goes. The color of the distinctions should be lighter and have a pink tint, also the cuff flaps should be pink. The plume should not be attached..

Carabinier Regiment, Carabinier

The two regiments were united as a brigade and assigned to the 12th Cavalry Division. As a unit they had a strength of 850 officers and enlisted men. On June 16, they were united with the corps under Marshal Ney at Quatre-Bras but did not see action. At Waterloo they took up positions in the second rank of the front line but remained only as a reserve until late afternoon. Only during the last cuirassier attacks at about 6:00 p.m. did they move against the squares without significant success.

Uniform: Well implemented, but there should not be a sun emblem on the cuirass, as it was intended only for officers. The cuffs were not pointed.

Foot Artillery, Officer

Uniform: Lyall had incorrectly assigned this officer of the light infantry, which however had white metal buttons and white piping. His depiction shows an the parade coat of a foot artillery officer; the officer's dress uniform according to the regulations of 1812, which, in addition to the infantry, also applied to parts of the light cavalry as well as the technical troops. The closed lapels can be seen well, but with the wrong number of buttons (five instead of seven). The light unit officers wore pants with their rank chevrons plus short boots. Source: after the 1812 series of plates by Carle Vernet.

Horse Artillery, Gunner

Twelve mounted batteries with 72 guns were assigned to the Northern Army for the 1815 campaign. On June 18, the artillery saw action with the large battery with over 80 guns at the opening and the preparation for the d'Erlon Corps' infantry assault. After the advance's failure, British cavalry pursued the retreating infantry and advanced to the French batteries, killing the gun crews.

Uniform: The shako plate would have been a semi-circular shield with crossed cannon barrels. The pointed cuffs had a red basic color and buttons set more to the back of the sleeve. Source: from an 1812 series of plates by Carle Vernet.

Horse Artillery, Trumpeter

Uniform: Like all musicians, the drummers or trumpeters of the artillery wore the livree as a distinguishing feature. There were two variants for them, with and without lapels, although in 1815 the simpler version with a row of buttons was used more. For it, the laces on the breast seam were decorated with the emblems. However, it is mentioned that also the simple and easier to obtain yellow laces were used, as shown in this illustration with sleeve chevrons. The trousers were always in blue for the artillery and in the field were mostly long overalls. The trumpet cord would have been braided in green and yellow.

Artillery Train, Driver

The train had several subdivisions. The main force was the artillery train, which was responsible for transporting and positioning the guns as well as the wagons. The baggage train *(Train d'Équipages)* was responsible for transporting the baggage and food. However, on 18 June, it was still stuck at Charleroi and was looted during the subsequent retreat.

Uniform: This representation dates more from the period 1804 to 1812 and corresponds more to the Train of the Guard. In 1815, the coattails were short, the distinctions were dark blue piped with white; for the Baggage Train in red-brown. The shoulder straps had a steel-blue base color with white piping. The suspension of the saber and the cartridge pouch is correct; however the pouch had no fittings. Either tall, cuffed boots or long overalls in the coat's color were worn in the field.

Engineers of the Line, Sapper

The engineer detachments of the 1st and 3rd Regiments were distributed among the infantry divisions in 1815 and were to assist in the removal of obstacles. However, since there were no classical engineer tasks in this battle, they were employed with the infantry in the attack to bolster its firepower. For example, the 1st Regiment's detachments, along with other units, stormed the main gate of La Haye Sainte.

Uniform: Overall, the appearance is correctly reproduced, but here, too, the lapels should be closed and the coattails short. The cuff flaps were made of black cloth. The shako is not likely to have cording, trim or the eagle badge. Either tall, cuffed boots or long overalls in the coat's color were worn.

ON THE FOLLOWING PAGES:

Units of the Imperial Guard, which ceased to exist in 1815

signed by

Charles Lyall
1894

Grenadiers Hollandaise of the Imperial Guard, Drummer

After the 1810 annexation of the Kingdom of Holland, on September 13, 1810, Napoleon ordered the integration of the Dutch Guard Infantry Regiment into the Imperial Guard. There it initially took the number 2, with formation of a second grenadier regiment it took the number 3. In the Russian campaign almost the entire regiment was captured, so that on February 15, 1813, the Dutch Grenadiers were disbanded.

Uniform: The drummer shown here is broadly similar in appearance to that prescribed for Dutch grenadiers. However, their fur caps had no metal plate and the braids on collars, lapels, cuff flaps and turnbacks were striped in red and gold. The scarlet epaulettes were to resemble those of the other Guard Grenadier drummers with yellow stripes on the sliders.

Grenadiers Hollandaise of the Imperial Guard, Drum Major

The drum major of the 3rd Grenadier Regiment of the Imperial Guard was an imposing and well-known figure. His name was Siliakus, who was 28 years old when he joined the Imperial Guard regiment and measured 2.02 meters tall. The regimental band he led included 30 drummers, 20 pipers and 14 oboists.

Uniform: The richly decorated uniform of a sky-blue coat and white pants with silver braid with Hungarian knots is well rendered in Lyall's depiction. The black busby, however, was adorned by a white plume with a sky-blue base and three white feathers, as well as the yellow bag and silver-colored cording correctly depicted here. The fringes on the tops of the boots were silver colored. The baton is incorrectly depicted because it had silver-colored metal parts and cords. Also the bandelier is described and depicted in other representations as having a rich silver fringe.

Grenadiers Hollandaise of the Imperial Guard, Piper

Uniform: The Dutch Grenadiers' regimental musicians were dressed in a sky-blue coat and black busby. The collar, cuffs, pointed cuff flaps, turnbacks, and lapels were yellow and trimmed with silver braid. The lapels are somewhat poorly drawn here, as the laces were closer together at the top, also the silver braids on the lapels were not curved but cut straight. The epaulettes should be silver "trèfle" (trefoils). The busby is correctly depicted except for the plume holder which was actually silver-colored.

Fusiliers-Chasseurs of the Imperial Guard, Fusilier

The imperial decree of September 19, 1806 directed the forming of the new "Middle Guard" with the Fusiliers-Grenadiers and the Fusiliers-Chasseurs. After the dissolution of the Imperial Guard, the Fusiliers-Chasseurs Regiment was incorporated into the *Corps royal des Chasseurs à pied de France* on July 1, 1814.

Uniform: Lyall shows the uniform mostly correctly, however, there are errors with the collar, cuffs and epaulettes. The collar should be completely blue without the white edging; the red cuffs are missing the white piping, and the crescent on the epaulettes should also be red.

Fusiliers-Grenadiers of the Imperial Guard, Fusilier

Along with the Fusiliers-Chasseurs shown in the previous plate, the Fusiliers-Grenadiers Regiment formed the "Middle Guard" and was incorporated into the *Corps royal des Grenadiers à pied de France* on July 1, 1814, when the Imperial Guard was disbanded.

Uniform: Lyall based this on a depiction from Vernet-Lami's 1822 series, which shows a fusilier in marching order from 1810. However, he has made some mistakes in the depiction, for example, the turnbacks conspicuously end flush with the coat lapels at the bottom and do not have any white eagle shown. Completely white epaulettes, which only have two red stripes on the bars, would be correct. The red cuffs should have white cuff flaps with three tips. The red pompom would have to be higher on the shako. The knapsack would have to have straps and the short saber was actually the "Sabre briquet" with a single knuckle guard.

Flanqueurs Grenadiers of the Imperial Guard, Flanqueur

The formation of a regiment of *"Flanqueurs"* of the Imperial Guard, which was assigned to the Young Guard was decreed on September 4, 1811. It was to be recruited from, among others, sons of *"Gardes généraux"* and *"Gardes forestiers"*, i.e. from foresters - this is probably where the green color of the coat came from. The regiment, which had been engaged in several battles, was disbanded in 1814 and the remaining soldiers were distributed among line units.

Uniform: In depicting the collet, Lyall made some errors in his interpretation of a plate by Vernet-Lami. The (narrower) piping on the lapels did not go along the bottom, and the red turnbacks were piped yellow (there were white eagles on the turnbacks). Also, the pointed cuffs would have been red, although the yellow piping is correct. The shako would have to have V-shaped strips on the sides, the color arrangement of the pompom is actually reversed.

Napoleon's Guides, Officer Around 1799–1800

Napoleon had already created a "bodyguard", for the Italian campaign in 1796, which also went with him to Egypt as "Guides". Then with the formating of the Consular Guard and later Imperial Guard in 1804, they entered the Chasseurs à Cheval Regiment.

Uniform: This representation by Lyall corresponds most closely to the image of an officer of the Guides as they were equipped for the Egyptian campaign or for the formation of the Consular Guard in 1800. However, the artist has taken some liberties here. The green coat is correct, but the collar should be completely red and the lapels should be pointed at the bottom and merge into three narrow prongs at the top. The red pants should be richly decorated with gold on the thighs. The vest should actually be red with gold frogging and braid. The crossed gold cords on the busby are confirmed by a portrait by Eugène de Beauharnais for 1800.

1st *Regiment Éclaireurs* of the Imperial Guard, Soldier of the Old Guard 1814

On December 9, 1813, Napoleon ordered the raising of three regiments of *Éclaireurs* (Scouts) for his Imperial Guard. The first two regiments were to be recruited from soldiers of the line cavalry, the third regiment from Polish cavalrymen. They were to be attached to the existing regiments of the Imperial Guard, the 1st to the Horse Grenadiers, the 2nd to the Dragoons and the 3rd to the Polish *Chevaulegers-Lanciers*. The *Éclaireur* regiments existed only for a short time and were disbanded by decree of May 12, 1814.

Uniform: The Old Guard soldier dressed in a hussar uniform is largely correctly depicted here. However, the dolman's pointed cuffs would have to be red. The overalls with leather reinforcement and red outer stripes are correct but the piping indicated on the pocket ran under the buttons and was also red. Some depictions also show gray overalls with leather trim. The leather straps on the otherwise correctly depicted shako are not documented, and the shako was usually secured with brass chin scales.

2nd *Regiment Éclaireurs* of the Imperial Guard, Soldier 1814

The 2nd Regiment of *Éclaireurs* was attached to the Dragoons of the Imperial Guard and half of it was to be armed with lances. The other half of the regiment was equipped with carbines.

Uniform: Soldiers of the 2nd Éclaireurs wore a single-breasted green coat with short coattails and crimson distinctions. However, the turnbacks ended flush with the tails at the bottom. The correctly shown white metal buttons were, however, decorated by an "à la Soubise" crimson border. The shoulder straps would have to be green with crimson piping. The tall shako, as shown here, had a crimson cloth cover, but no eagle plate on it, but only a cockade and the green pompom above it. The yellow border is confirmed in only a few depictions, but not in the Vernet-Lami series more commonly used by Lyall.

1st *Regiment Gardes d'Honneurs* of the Imperial Guard, Soldier in Parade Uniform

After the defeat of the Grand Army in Russia, Napoleon wanted to create a unit that would give the sons of the nobility and the French upper class direct access to the Imperial Guard, in a project similar to that of the *Gendarmes d'Ordonnance* in 1806/1807. Therefore, on April 3, 1813, four regiments of *Gardes d'Honneur* were formed, recruited from various administrative districts.

Uniform: The four regiments were uniformly dressed in Hussar uniforms, distinguished by the regimental number on the shako plate and the color of the plume's tip. Lyall here shows the appearance of the honor guards, but with errors in the colors. The fur trim was actually black, the collar and cuffs as well as the pants were scarlet and not the crimson as shown here. The cords of the barrel sash are correctly shown in crimson. The sabretache should bear the regimental number under the eagle and the straps should be white, like the other leather gear.

Gardes d'Honneurs of the Imperial Guard, Officer in Field Uniform

The four regiments of *Gardes d'Honneur*, after being formed by an imperial decree of 29 July 1813, were assigned to the Imperial Guard. On September 6, 1813, Napoleon ordered that the 1st Regiment be attached to the Chasseurs à Cheval, the 2nd to the Dragoons, the 3rd to the Horse Grenadiers, and the 4th to the Lancers. At the end of 1813, the *Gardes d'Honneur* lost their Guard status and formed a division in two brigades. However, a decree of 24 June 1814 then ordered the regiments to be disbanded.

Uniform: The officer shown here is correctly depicted with the - actually black - busby and red bag with silver decoration. The plume, however, should be green with the tip colored according to the regiment. The pelisse had black fur trim and for the officers it had silver-colored buttons, frogging and laces. The overalls are also correctly shown with silver outer stripes, but for officers these are usually shown with double braid, without attached buttons and without leather reinforcing.

Selected bibliography

As in the previous volumes, recommendations for more in-depth reading are given here. For a description of the Battle of Waterloo, please refer to the list in the first volume of the series.

Literature on the French Army 1815

The following list identifies the relevant recent works that were primarily used for the text of this volume and evaluation of Lyall's plates.

- Beaufort, Louis de: Waterloo, series of plates with 48 sheets, 1966.
- Catchpol, Stanley: "The Dress of the French Army during the Waterloo Campaign", Tradition, London, no year.
- Courcelle, Patrice et al: Les Carnets de la Campagne. Currently 15 issues since 1999.
- Dawson, Paul L.: Napoleon's Waterloo Army - Uniforms and Equipment, (Barnsley: Frontline Books, 2019).
- Haythornthwaite, Philip, The Uniforms of the Battle of Waterloo (Munich: Heyne, 1976).
- Haythornthwaite, Philip, Uniforms of Waterloo (Poole: Blandford, 1974).
- Haythornthwaite, Philip, Waterloo Armies, Men, Organization and Tactics (Barnsley, 2007).
- Juhel, Pierre: La Garde Impériale pendant les Cent-Jours (1815). With plates by Keith Rocco and Peter Bunde. Published by La Revue Napoleon, Annecy-le-Vieux 2009.
- Klimek, St. J., "Waterloo - Die französische Nordarmee", Die Zinnfigur, Uniformhefte Nos. 7 and 10, (Lehrte, no year).
- Klimek, St. J., "Die Uniformierung der französischen Kavallerie unter Napoleon I" in Die Zinnfigur, Uniformheft 17 (Lehrte, no year).
- Knötel, Richard, Große Uniformkunde, Volumes 1-8 (Rathenow, 1890-1914); see online at http://uniformenportal.de/index.php?/category/102.
- Riehn, Richard K., The French Imperial Army, The Campaign of 1813-1814 and Waterloo (New York, 1973).
- Rousselot, Lucien, Armée Francaise, 106 plates. German translation published by Zeughaus Verlag under the title "Napoleons Armee 1800-1815", Berlin 2010; English translation published as Napoleon's Army 1790-1815 (Philadelphia: Casemate, 2010).
- Thiriar, James; Meganck, Paul, Les Uniformes de Waterloo 1815 (Brussels, 2007).

On the French infantry in 1815 and their inadequate equipment, an article appears at Napoleon Online at http://www.napoleon-online.de/armee_frankreich_infanterie1815.html.

Depictions and original pieces relating to the French Army in 1815 can be studied at the Napoleon Online's Uniform Portal at http://uniformenportal.de/index.php?/tags/1-l_frankreich/48-1815

Four volumes have been published in the series
"Uniforms of the Armies of Waterloo":

- British Army from 1815, with 75 plates
- Allied Armies from 1815, with 56 plates
- Prussian Army from 1815, with 39 plates
- French Army of 1815, with 70 plates

Orders can be placed through brick-and-mortar
and online bookstores.